Dodge
Returns
to
NASCAR

UMI Publications Staff

President and Publisher: **Ivan Mothershead;** Vice President and Associate Publisher: **Charlie Keiger;** Associate Publisher: **Rick Peters;** Controller: **Lewis Patton;** National Advertising Manager: **Mark Cantey;** Advertising Executive: **Paul Kaperonis;** Managing Editor: **Ward Woodbury;** Associate Editor: **Gary McCredie;** Senior Editor: **Bob Kelly;** Art Director: **Brett Shippy;** Senior Designer: **Paul Bond;** Manager of Information Systems: **Chris Devera;** Administrative Staff: **Mary Flowe, Dorothy Gates, Linda Goltz, Sean McCartney, Christin Petrasko, Joanie Tarbert**

Dodge Returns to NASCAR is Officially Licensed by Dodge and NASCAR.

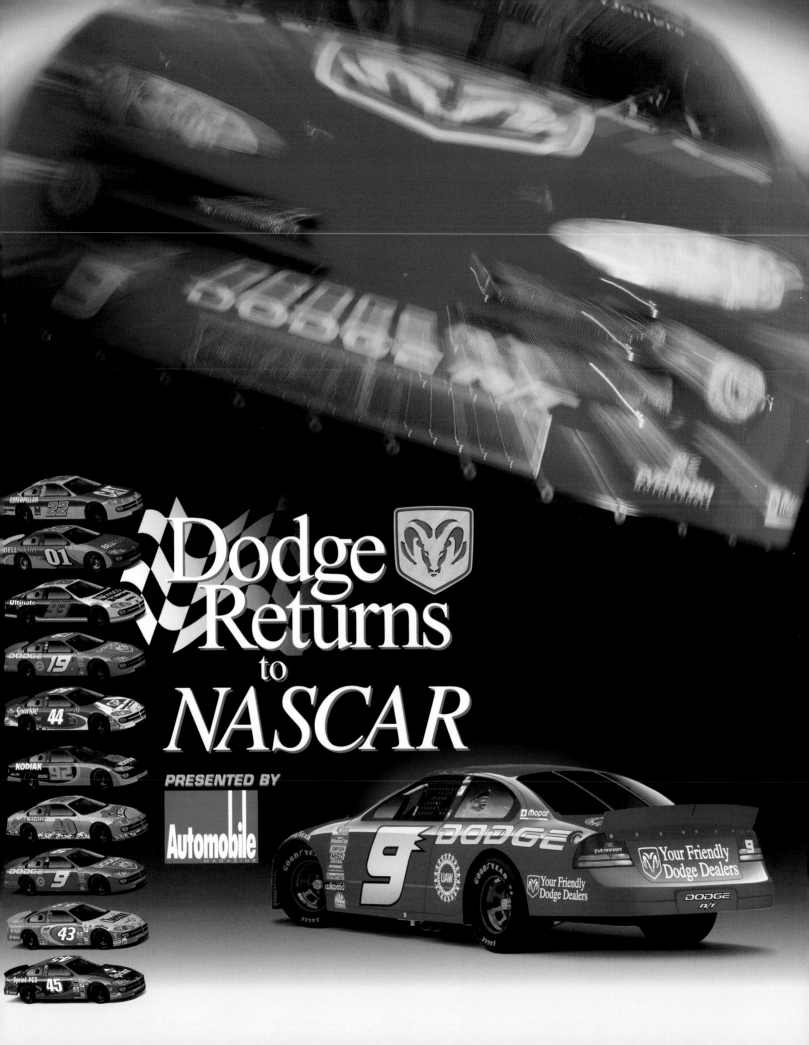

Dodge Returns to NASCAR

It's a long way from Auburn Hills, Michigan, to Daytona Beach, Florida. In fact it takes 494 days to complete the journey effectively. It takes five top-drawer Winston Cup racing teams, a cadre of Dodge engineers, almost three thousand dedicated Dodge dealers, and some of the most advanced product development technology in the automotive world.

Or, in brief, it takes a Dodge team, a group of determined people employing the same kind of strategy that we use to build vehicles like Durango, Ram, Intrepid, Viper, and the rest. We call it a platform team. And it's a way of utilizing an organization's best resources to achieve what may at first glance seem nearly impossible.

Yet the platform team approach is just one of the advances Dodge has brought to the Winston Cup arena. In these pages you can read the rest of the story. You'll learn what's different about the Dodge approach to motorsports. How, in one sense, we've actually turned back the clock and built a factory racing team that is actually a factory effort, not just a factory-funded effort. And, in another sense, how we've jumped ahead in time and applied some of our state-of-the-art development technology to race-car building. How we've networked the race teams and factory engineers to form what is best described as a virtual garage. How we've brought lots of smart people together without having to physically bring them together.

It's all here. It's different, and it's Dodge. I hope you enjoy reading about our 494-day journey as much as we've enjoyed taking it.

Sincerely,

Jim Julow
Vice President
Dodge Division

DODGE RETURNS TO NASCAR!

We all know the power and the glory of automobile racing, NASCAR style. Cable television viewers can find NASCAR news and NASCAR racing on their screens around the clock. NASCAR is a major presence on the Internet. NASCAR is on the radio. There's nothing quite like it anywhere else in the wide world of automobile racing, and there isn't a major racing series in the civilized world that doesn't envy NASCAR's growth, as well as its ability to attract and hold masses of loyal fans for what is now a year-round season. This is a major American success story.

It's another kind of success story at the same time. For fifty years Southern legislators, Southern politicians, Southern media, and Southern chambers of commerce have tried to sell the idea of a dynamic new American South. They had ample reason to do so, because the American North was rigidly and reflexively prejudiced against the South. A Southern accent was a sign of stupidity. Entertainers like Dorothy Loudon, Stan Freeberg, and Tom Lehrer regularly brought houses down with satire that couldn't have been used against any other regional or ethnic group in American society. As a Kentuckian, born to an undeniably Southern family, I longed for some countervailing force, some strong Southern phenomenon that might open some cynical eyes and show a wider American audience what we were all about.

And then, along came Bill France, Sr., and stock car racing. Southern cities, Southern accents, Southern style, along with the uniquely Southern excitement of big-time stock car racing, have established bridgeheads in the non-Southern United States that would make old Marse Robert E. Lee grin like a fox. NASCAR is national now! NASCAR has come to town and millions of people—eyes wide open and fingers in their ears—are getting the message. Bill France, Sr., certainly didn't intend to capture our hearts and minds for anything except the wonder and excitement of stock car racing, but stock car racing has developed a cultural dynamic all its own. It's a media juggernaut, and it's changing all the old stereotypes just as it changed all of our television viewing habits.

If you were the Dodge Division of DaimlerChrysler and you had already blazed a trail of success through stock car racing in the Fifties and Sixties, wouldn't you want to dive back into NASCAR and show the world your best stuff? Absolutely! And that's exactly what Dodge has been preparing to do for the past year. The energies and intellects of hundreds of Dodge engineers and designers and managers—not to mention almost 3000 highly motivated Dodge dealers—are focused on the debut of the new Dodge Intrepid R/T Winston Cup cars at the Daytona 500. This special book chronicles that return to stock car racing and will attempt to give you a comprehensive look at what it takes to start with a clean sheet of paper and mount a full-scale assault on the Winston Cup series. And if, along the way, we give you a taste of the unique drama and color of this great sport, so much the better.

It was determined that I would serve as editor and Larry

Crane would be the graphic designer. AUTOMOBILE MAGA-ZINE's managing editor, Amy Skogstrom, would keep us on time and within sight of the budget. We assembled a team of knowledgeable enthusiasts who are also professional journalists and parceled out the assignments. Writers Eddie Alterman, Reilly Brennan, Kevin Clemens, Preston Lerner, Michael Jordan, William Neely, and Joe Schulte would handle the heavy lifting. Bill Neely, especially, was a welcome addition to our team. Bill worked with NASCAR as a Goodyear PR man in the Sixties and co-authored *Stand On It!*—perhaps the funniest and best book ever written about racing—with our late pal Bob Ottum. We were incredibly fortunate to get David Kimble to do a set of his brilliant cut-away drawings, the centerpiece of which appears on page 42. William Livingston handled the bulk of our photography, but we received a lot of help—and a lot of photographs—from the NASCAR archives in Daytona Beach.

We were proud, pleased, and perfectly amazed to be given the opportunity to create this book. We've all lived and breathed motorsports since we were too young to drive, and we all hurled ourselves into the task. We sincerely hope that you enjoy it.

David E. Davis, Jr.
Founder and Editor Emeritus
Automobile Magazine

The 2001 Daytona 500 marks Dodge's return to NASCAR's most prestigious series; Dodge last ran a Winston Cup race in 1985.

GEORGE TIEDEMANN

THE TECH CENTER
GOES RACING

Think of it as a race shop with 5.2 million square feet of space and 12,000 engineers. By Michael Jordan

Car manufacturers have been involved in stock car racing almost from the very moment that NASCAR competition officially got under way back in 1948. But the role that the DaimlerChrysler Technical Center has played in the launch of Dodge's new Winston Cup teams is like nothing that could have been imagined fifty years ago.

When Chrysler first went NASCAR racing in 1955, all it had to do was to keep sending fresh parts to millionaire Carl Kiekhaefer and his Mercury Outboard–sponsored team. Kiekhaefer's brace of Chrysler 300s with their first-generation Hemi engines dominated NASCAR in 1955 and 1956 by winning forty-nine of the 101 events they entered, a standard of preparation and performance that went unmatched for a decade. As the Sixties arrived, factory support focused on engines, and Chrysler's second-generation Hemi helped Richard Petty become acknowledged as the king of stock car racing in 1967, when his Plymouth Satellite GTX won twenty-seven races, including ten in a row.

It takes more than just parts to win Winston Cup races these days, however. It takes technology—the science of speed. And few places in the world are as well-equipped to explore the science of speed as the DaimlerChrysler Tech Center. Built on a 504-acre site in Auburn Hills, Michigan, some thirty miles north of Detroit, the Tech Center incorporates design, engineering, prototype production, and test facilities under a single roof. It's one of the largest buildings in North America, with some 5.2 million square feet of working space. More than 12,000 people work here, surely the largest concentration of engineering talent on the planet.

Tim Culbertson, the program manager for the Dodge Winston Cup program, notes that the teams involved in the NASCAR program were immediately impressed by the Tech Center's facilities. "When we were first introducing ourselves to different teams, they all toured this facility," Culbertson says. "During some of my early racing experiences in other programs, some teams would be awfully skeptical of facto-

ry engineering. 'We don't need that stuff,' they'd say. But one of the things that I'm really excited about is the way the Winston Cup teams understood the possible use of this building right away. They've been early adopters, as it were, and they've seen the Tech Center as an advantage."

Ray Evernham, team principal of Evernham Motorsports, confirms his enthusiasm for the resources offered by the Tech Center. "One of the things I was looking for when I was forming my own race team was a close relationship with a manufacturer," he says. "A place like the Tech Center helps not just with technology but also in getting things done quicker. And it gets done to a uniform standard of very high quality, which is what you must have to make it in NASCAR racing today. I'm not aware of another team that built a Winston Cup car from the ground up in 500 days. It's one thing to build a new race car from existing parts, but something else again to build a race car with a new engine, chassis, and body style."

Culbertson confirms that the Tech Center has had a significant impact on the progress of the Dodge Winston Cup program. He says, "I'm very, very proud of our use of the CATIA CAD/CAM computer software in the engine program. It's been a tremendous effort to get this program up to speed. Keep in mind that back in November 1999, this engine was just a glimmer in our eye. We released the design of the engine in December 1999, had metal castings by February 2000, had a running engine by May, and were on the track by June. What you see in this Dodge program are what I like to call engineering athletes, people who are doing things in a matter of months that would ordinarily take two or three years in the course of making a production car."

Culbertson also reports that an entire range of science from the Tech Center has been used to develop the new Dodge Winston Cup car. He says, "We've used our capability in Computational Fluid Dynamics to develop the engine intakes. We've used a special computerized program to help cast the engines, so we can make sure the hot metal flows and sets up without any flaws that could cause a fail-

At DaimlerChrysler's Tech Center, the design, engineering, prototyping, and testing of the new Dodge racing car are centralized under one massive roof. The building sits on a 504-acre site, comprises 5.2 million square feet, and houses an engineering staff of 12,000.

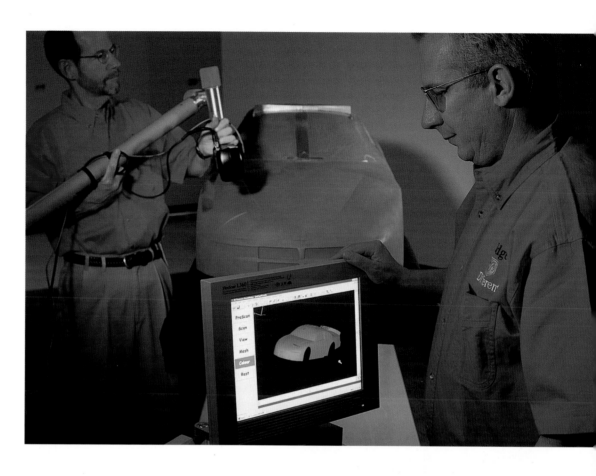

Above: Timothy Duff (left) and Don Misson of Dodge with the 3/8-scale version of the Intrepid Winston Cup car. The body of the car is shaped by its own set of computer based tools distinct from those used on the chassis. Right: The FDM 2000, a tool that facilitates quick production of prototype parts.

ure. In the wind tunnel, our use of 3/8-scale models of the car bodies instead of the 1/5-scale used by other manufacturers is cutting edge, as is our use of Computational Fluid Dynamics. On the chassis side, we're making use of our simulation capabilities, some that are our own technologies and some in which we've been instrumental in designing the application."

The link between the DaimlerChrysler Tech Center in Michigan and the race shops of the NASCAR teams is far from a one-way street, however. Stock car racing is about speed on the track, but it also calls for speed away from the track. Technology must be developed quickly and parts produced on time, because the green flag falls on Sunday afternoon and there's no waiting around for a car that's not ready. In racing, timeliness is crucial. Moreover, there's no way to disguise engineering performance, because it's measured right out in the open, where it can be understood as easily as a few hundredths of a second in a qualifying lap or the order of finish at the end of 500 miles. NASCAR's Winston Cup championship series is the fiercest, most unrelenting engineering challenge of all. It's almost like launching a moon rocket some thirty-four weekends a year. As a result, DaimlerChrysler's engineers have become smarter

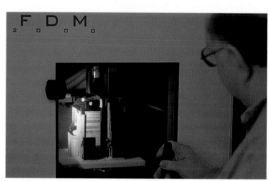

and faster, and they have an even keener appreciation for quality and performance.

Culbertson confirms that the scope of such an engineering challenge has had a noticeable affect on the people at the Tech Center. "Don't think that Winston Cup racing is low technology. It's actually very high tech, but it's just not glamorous technology. You have to remember that not everybody at the Tech Center works on things like anti-lock brakes or traction control or fuel-injection. Some people work on strength of materials, or they work on something as simple as turning a flat piece of metal into a round piece of metal. And a lot of the technologies we've been bridging between race engineering and production engineering have been base technologies, the kind of thing you see in Engineering 101.

"For example, we had a minor setback in our engine program, the kind of thing that happens in any engineering challenge, and we brought in our experts in finite element analysis, the Tech Center people who are basically just trying to make things stronger. They confirmed that we had identified the right problem and saw that the solution we mapped out was correct. And then they thanked us. They said, 'We like dealing with you. We came up with a proposed fix and within nine days, you had it made and ready. We don't usually get that kind of turnaround in production cars. We have confidence in our tools, but usually it takes a long time to get verification. You guys gave us instant verification.'"

As it turns out, racing is the perfect crucible for young engineers. Racing is basically much simpler than production engineering because concerns about durability and cost are simplified, and ideas can become three-dimensional realities in a much shorter period of time. DaimlerChrysler engineers also are able to quickly adapt to the demands of racing

because they already employ a platform engineering approach to car design, in which small teams take a responsibility for the entire car. "With platform engineering, you design systems, not just individual parts," Culbertson says. "And to my way of thinking, the ultimate system is an entire car. So with the platform approach to a race car, the engineers can learn all about aerodynamics, all about chassis, and all about engines. You might be an engine guy, but you're still learning about chassis and you're still learning about aero, and you get all of it at a real fast pace."

The DaimlerChrysler Technical Center's involvement in NASCAR Winston Cup competition pays off for everyone involved. The five development teams can boast access to the kind of technological resources that previously were associated only with Formula 1 racing—all the aerodynamic testing, all the chassis simulations, and all the engine science in a racing car that costs $100,000 instead of $1 million. At the same time, DaimlerChrysler gets an incredibly intense arena in which to educate and train its engineers, helping them to develop a respect for performance, durability, and safety that will carry over into the production of everyday cars and trucks. ∎

A model of the Dodge NASCAR Winston Cup car undergoes testing in the Tech Center's slotted-wall wind tunnel; the 3/8-scale tunnel's 1200-horsepower fan is able to replicate speeds approaching 180 mph— helpful for fine-tuning the shape of the car before expensive full-scale testing begins.

BACK TO DAYTONA

Dodge returns to Winston Cup racing. By Preston Lerner

**Left to right: Team owners Ray
Evernham, Bill Davis, and Kyle Petty,
along with Dodge's Lou Patane,
pose with the brand-new,
as-yet-unapproved Intrepid R/T.**

When the history books are written, the Cracker Barrel Old Country Store 500 at the Atlanta Motor Speedway in March 1999 won't be remembered for anything that transpired on the track. No, the weekend's most memorable event occurred after the race, far from prying eyes and wagging tongues, in a Ritz-Carlton room booked under a false name.

There, top Dodge executives hatched a bold plan to bring DaimlerChrysler's performance marque back to NASCAR Winston Cup racing. The engineering was doable, they insisted, the marketing opportunities limitless. But Dodge didn't intend to go racing the old-fashioned way, with the bulk of the decisions, technology, and money coming from the factory. As Lou Patane, vice-president of motorsports operations, puts it: "We wanted to do it our own way—in a word, differently."

The Dodge difference was a revolutionary concept that called for the factory and its race teams to work as partners, sharing information up until the moment the green flag waved. This so-called one-team approach was modeled directly on the platform-team philosophy Chrysler had embraced to bring passenger cars from concept to market with remarkable speed.

A version of the one-team concept had already paid dividends in NASCAR's Craftsman Truck Series. Now, the company wanted to take the program onward and upward—upward to Winston Cup and onward to include the dealers who would sell on Monday when a Dodge won on Sunday. In fact, Dodge was so committed to this idea that it decided to return to Winston Cup only if its dealers—every one of them—agreed to pony up a hefty chunk of change to support the program.

Which is why ten of the company's most prominent dealers—members of the Dodge Dealer Advertising Association Executive Committee—had been invited to Atlanta for a chance to see, feel, hear, touch, and smell the mighty magic that's made NASCAR one of the country's most potent sports-marketing phenomena. Several of them were already race fans. Some were racers themselves. But all of them were clear-eyed, hard-nosed businessmen, and they were worried about the program's projected costs (substantial) and potential pitfalls (ditto). At one point, Carl Galeana, owner of Van Dyke Dodge in Warren, Michigan, and an accomplished SCCA racer, demanded point-blank: "Will NASCAR allow Dodge to be competitive?"

"Look," NASCAR chief operating officer Mike Helton replied, "we're not the WWF." But as Helton fleshed out his position, it became clear to the dealers that NASCAR didn't want to see Dodge fall on its face. "We were satisfied that our cars weren't just going to be billboards running in circles around the track," Galeana says.

When the last question had been asked, Jim Julow, Dodge Division vice-president, posed one of his own: Would the dealers commit enough of their local advertising money to serve as the primary sponsor of Dodge's two factory cars? "If I get ten thumbs-up," he told them, "we go ahead with the program. If I get seven, that's it, we're finished. It's all or nothing."

The vote was unanimous: ten to zero. Dodge was on the road that would lead to the Daytona 500 in 2001.

Granted, there were still numerous hurdles to over-

NASCAR newcomer Chip Ganassi officially commits his BellSouth and Coors Light cars to Dodge's Winston Cup program for 2001. With this announcement, Chip Ganassi Racing with Felix Sabates becomes Dodge's fifth and final development team and raises the number of new Intrepid R/T Cup cars to ten.

come before the wraps were taken off the new millennium Winston Cup effort during a glitzy unveiling at the Waldorf-Astoria in midtown Manhattan on October 14, 1999. As Julow explains: "The program could have gone south plenty of places along the way." The executive committee's vote had to be confirmed by the boards of Dodge's thirty-nine Dealer Advertising Associations, then approved by all 2900-plus Dodge dealers. And all the votes were contingent upon getting a proven name—Ray Evernham, as it turned out—to ramrod the program.

But once the ready-for-liftoff call was made, the program moved faster than, well, an Intrepid R/T on the high banks of Talladega. Initially, Evernham Motorsports, Petty Enterprises, and Bill Davis Racing were signed as development teams. Later, unexpectedly, Melling Racing and Chip Ganassi Racing with Felix Sabates joined the fold,

which will give Dodge a total of ten cars when Daytona opens for practice in February.

This isn't dipping a toe in the water. It's arriving with a splash. Patane, in fact, is expecting top-ten finishes right off the bat. "I know it sounds brazen," he admits. "But the platform-team approach has been extremely successful extremely quickly." Or as Evernham has said: "I'm not expecting to win the Daytona 500. But I'm not expecting not to win it, either."

In retrospect, Dodge's return to Winston Cup seems to have been inevitable. The desperate financial crises of the Seventies had forced Chrysler out of the motorsports arena during the Eighties. But as the company's bottom line improved, a new generation of Dodge products sped into victory lanes in SCCA club races, the North American Touring Car Championship, NHRA drag races, World of

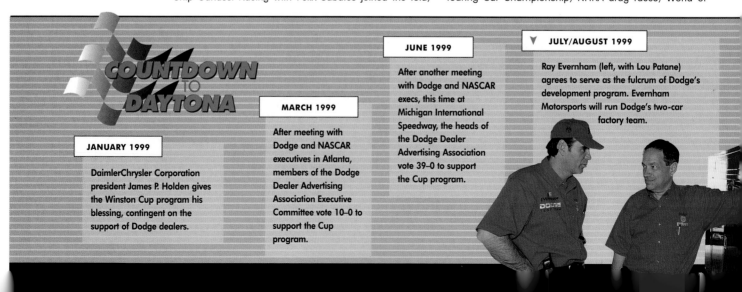

COUNTDOWN TO DAYTONA

JANUARY 1999

DaimlerChrysler Corporation president James P. Holden gives the Winston Cup program his blessing, contingent on the support of Dodge dealers.

MARCH 1999

After meeting with Dodge and NASCAR executives in Atlanta, members of the Dodge Dealer Advertising Association Executive Committee vote 10–0 to support the Cup program.

JUNE 1999

After another meeting with Dodge and NASCAR execs, this time at Michigan International Speedway, the heads of the Dodge Dealer Advertising Association vote 39–0 to support the Cup program.

JULY/AUGUST 1999

Ray Evernham (left, with Lou Patane) agrees to serve as the fulcrum of Dodge's development program. Evernham Motorsports will run Dodge's two-car factory team.

Outlaws sprint car extravaganzas, and, most gloriously, the 24 Hours of Le Mans.

By 1996, Dodge felt confident enough to return to NASCAR, where the Craftsman Truck Series gave the company a chance to hone its unproved one-team approach in a not-quite-ready-for-prime-time environment. The rookie season was predictably rocky. But Dodge trucks won two races in 1997 and two more in 1998 while generating plenty of speculation.

Most observers had assumed that the truck effort was merely a prelude to Dodge's return to Winston Cup racing. Not true, Dodge officials insist. "That was not even an inkling in our mind," Julow says. "And, frankly, I'm not sure we could have gone Winston Cup racing even if we'd wanted to."

Chrysler's merger with Daimler-Benz, announced in May 1998 and finalized the following November, prompted some serious corporate soul-searching. Meetings regarding brand strategy brought Dodge's position as Chrysler's performance marque into sharper focus and nudged the company's motorsports program in a new direction. "We realized that if we were going to go racing," Julow says, "we ought to get our butts in Winston Cup."

By January 1999, DaimlerChrysler was ready to rumble—if its dealers voted in favor of the program. The let's-go-racing bandwagon played the dealer circuit through the summer, and the last of the dealer commitments were made in September. By the time of the Waldorf-Astoria announcement in October, the Winston Cup program was already ramping up.

Thanks to the Craftsman Truck Series, Dodge already had a cadre of seasoned racing veterans in place—NASCAR program manager Bob Wildberger, engineering lead Tim Culbertson, and engine guru Ted Flack, to name just a few. Job openings were posted and filled immediately. "We are a very lean organization," Patane says. "We probably have 30 percent of the people that our competitors have. That's because we don't have a racing department here. We work in a platform-team environment."

Kyle Petty (left) and his crew with Ray Evernham (right) during track testing of the Intrepid R/T.

AUGUST 1999	SEPTEMBER 1999

Richard and Kyle Petty meet with Dodge officials during the Cup race weekend at Michigan International Speedway and commit Petty Enterprises to the Dodge program.

The DAAs representing all 2900-plus Dodge dealers line up unanimously behind the Cup program. Richard Petty sparks a Craftsman Truck Series Dodge to life during the festivities at the Inn at Bay Harbor on Lake Michigan.

SEPTEMBER 1999

Crew chief Ray Evernham leaves Hendrick Motorsports in mid-season after winning Winston Cup championships with Jeff Gordon in 1995, 1997, and 1998.

FALL 1999

Bill Davis and core members of Bill Davis Racing visit Dodge's motorsports operations in Michigan and subsequently agree to become Dodge's third Winston Cup development team.

Traditionally, car companies have been structured around autonomous departments—design, marketing, production, and so on, each with its own hierarchy and concerns. As a new car is developed, it moves sequentially from one department to another. Besides taking a long time, this approach also tends to suffocate creativity. So when Dodge wanted to quickly transform its 1989 Viper show car into an equally exotic production vehicle, it gambled on the platform-team paradigm.

The Viper unveiled in 1991 was the product of a small, tight-knit corps—a platform team—drawn from each of the company's many disciplines. Bean-counters, therefore, were able to work with stylists from the inception of the program rather than first locking horns three years down the road. This allowed everybody to work faster, smarter,

cheaper, and it was the foundation of Chrysler's renaissance in the '90s.

The platform-team concept also came in handy on the racing front. Dodge faced a brutally steep learning curve when it entered the Craftsman Truck Series, the company's first factory foray into NASCAR in a generation. "The platform-team approach got us from Point A to Point B faster than the competition," Wildberger says.

In the racing world, the platform-team approach evolved into the one-team concept. Most manufacturers do most of their motorsports development in-house, then pass along their racing parts and insight to the teams using their equipment. But Dodge decided to make its race teams full partners in the development process, requiring them to exchange information not just with the

Below: Dodge hopes the motorsports world will see a sea of red blanketing the front of Winston Cup fields in 2001. Actually, only the two Evernham Intrepid R/Ts will race in red colors. But the all-for-one, one-for-all philosophy underlying Dodge's Winston Cup effort is displayed here, as members of the Evernham, Petty, and Davis development teams practice their victory-circle smiles.

COUNTDOWN TO DAYTONA

OCTOBER 1999

Five-hundred-day countdown to Daytona begins.

OCTOBER 1999

Dodge's imminent return to Winston Cup racing is announced during a glitzy unveiling at the Waldorf-Astoria Hotel in New York City.

OCTOBER 1999

The Dodge return-to-Winston-Cup news conference is reprised at the Talladega Superspeedway.

JANUARY 2000

A flame-red Dodge Intrepid R/T Winston Cup show car is unveiled at the North American International Auto Show in Detroit. None of the body templates have yet been approved by NASCAR, however.

For it's Winston Cup debut, Dodge planned to field three teams. But somebody had to serve as the centerpiece of the development program and lead the official Dodge factory team. It didn't take long for Dodge to identify its top choice—Ray Evernham.

factory but also with each other. In fact, each of them would be wired via T1 connections to the DaimlerChrysler Technology Center in Auburn Hills, Michigan, thereby creating a one-team virtual garage.

For its Winston Cup debut, Dodge planned to field three teams. But somebody had to serve as the centerpiece of the development program and lead the official Dodge factory team—two red Intrepids bearing sponsorship from Your Friendly Dodge Dealers. He had to be a proven winner, of course, but at the same time, he needed a profile high enough to give the entire effort some credibility. It didn't take long for Dodge to identify its top choice. "I'm not sure Ray Evernham is the only person who could have done it," Julow says. "But I believe he's the best person for the job."

Super-professional and mega-motivated, Evernham exemplified the new breed of Winston Cup crew chief. He first heard from Dodge in late 1998, while he and Jeff Gordon were winning their third NASCAR Winston Cup championship in four years. A long, bumpy she-loves-me-she-loves-me-not courtship followed. But by the summer of 1999, even as Dodge was about to launch its Cup program, the engagement seemed to be permanently off. Then, out of the blue, Evernham got a call from Lou Patane. "Ray," Patane said, "we've got to talk again."

This time around, Evernham didn't need much romancing. "It was what I needed in my life at that time," he explains. "I didn't want to be a crew chief anymore. But I didn't feel I could make a big difference in any other position at Hendrick Motorsports. Sure, it was hard to leave. But sometimes, when a tremendous opportunity comes your way, it comes with a price."

Although Evernham had expected to finish the season with Gordon, he was unceremoniously cut loose in September—an inglorious close to one of the most remarkable chapters in NASCAR history. The good news was that the firing gave Evernham some much-needed time to build his team. "When I left Hendrick," he recalls, "I didn't even have a desk."

Several of his ex-teammates, most notably chief mechanic Ed Guzzo, would eventually find their way to Evernham Motorsports. But Evernham needed lots of warm bodies—he expects to have 100 by Daytona—and he couldn't afford to be too choosy. "We've used a lot of inexperienced people, which is what we did with the 24 [Gordon] car," he says. "I go through a lot of people, honestly, before finding the right ones."

Evernham hired another Hendrick refugee, Ron

FEBRUARY 2000

At Daytona International Speedway, after months of intense media speculation, Dodge officially announces its initial slate of teams and drivers for 2001—John Andretti, Kyle Petty, and his son Adam for Petty Enterprises; Ward Burton and Dave Blaney for Bill Davis Racing; and two undisclosed drivers for Evernham Motorsports.

MARCH 2000

Unexpectedly, Dodge officials open discussions with team owners Mark Melling and Chip Ganassi about creating two more Dodge Cup teams in 2001.

MARCH 2000

Former Winston Cup champion Bill Elliott is named the driver of Evernham Motorsports #9 Intrepid R/T. As part of the deal, Elliott Racing will merge with Evernham Motorsports.

APRIL 2000

The first full-scale Intrepid R/T Cup car is tested in Lockheed's state-of-the-art wind tunnel in Georgia.

A Dodge program without its most famous icon was unthinkable.
In August 1999, King Richard and his son Kyle were asked
to join Dodge's Cup program. They didn't take long to answer.

Vicarro, to oversee engine development in the shop in Harrisburg, North Carolina, that had formerly housed the Evernham-Gordon Busch Series program. He also leased space in Mooresville, North Carolina. One of the first items he installed was a digital clock counting down the time to the start of the Daytona 500.

Evernham still needed two drivers, and one of them had to be—like him—a known quantity with star quality. "I talked to Bill Elliott as soon as I knew I was going to do the Dodge program," Evernham says. "He was perfect because his contract was up and he didn't have a sponsor, but he's still got some more championships in him."

In 2001, Elliott will once again be in a red #9—the number came courtesy of Melling Racing—and Elliott Racing will merge with Evernham Motorsports. Elliott will be joined by young Busch Series regular Casey Atwood. The similarities between the twenty-year-old phenom and Evernham's one-time protégé Jeff Gordon are by no means coincidental.

If Evernham was a coup for

Dodge, then Richard Petty was a given. After all, a Dodge program without its most famous icon was unthinkable. In August 1999, at Michigan International Speedway, Patane and Wildberger asked King Richard and his son Kyle to join Dodge's Cup program. They didn't have to wait long for an answer.

"All we had to do was work out the details," the elder Petty says. "We'd been waiting for it, okay? That was one of the reasons we'd gone with Dodge in the truck series, because we were hoping they'd get involved with Winston Cup. What drew us in was the promise of the technology we could tap into."

Long before its new Cup program was officially announced, the Pettys emptied a building that was being used as a storeroom in Level Cross, North Carolina, and transformed it into an R&D facility. R&D managers Doug Hewitt and Kurt Romberg, the son of an engineer who'd worked on the great Dodge Daytonas and Plymouth Superbirds of yore, were placed in charge of the program. In the existing engine shop, a new room was created so engine builder Keith Almond could work exclusively on the Dodge project.

Petty Enterprises planned to run three cars in 2001 for John Andretti, Kyle, and his nineteen-year-old son, Adam. Sadly, the promising youngster was killed during practice for a Busch Series event at New Hampshire Inter-

COUNTDOWN TO DAYTONA

MAY 2000
Adam Petty is killed during a Busch Series practice session at New Hampshire International Speedway in Loudon.

◄ **MAY 2000**
Kyle Petty (in blue) gives the Intrepid R/T its first track test at Homestead-Miami Speedway. The car is fitted with a high-compression version of Dodge's Craftsman Truck Series engine.

▲ **MAY 2000**
Casey Atwood (left), a nineteen-year-old Busch Series veteran, is named as teammate to Bill Elliott (center) in the Evernham Motorsports Dodge factory team.

The Dodge Cup engine makes its first dyno run.

▼ **MAY 2000**

national Speedway in May 2000. After a long driver search, Buckshot Jones, a Busch Series veteran with limited Cup experience, was named as the team's third driver.

Evernham and Petty gave Dodge lots of visibility but a marginal track record. Evernham was untried as an owner, and Petty Enterprises hadn't been a consistent front-runner since the King's heyday. So when it started auditioning candidates for its third development team, Dodge was determined to land a top ten outfit. More than a half-dozen team owners were invited to Michigan for quick meet-the-folks visits. One who stood out was Bill Davis, whose two-car team regularly ran up front even though it didn't carry the clout Richard Childress, Rick Hendrick, and Joe Gibbs enjoyed at General Motors.

Davis isn't the most effusive guy in the world, but he was pretty stoked when he returned to High Point, North Carolina, in the fall of 1999. "Everybody's got to go up there," he told his team. The next week, he and five core team members flew to Michigan for the grand tour of Dodge's motorsports operation. Everyone was sold on the program. But what clinched the deal was a lunchtime conversation Davis had with Kyle Petty at a local Mexican joint.

"Kyle and Ray were already on board," Davis recalls. "The fact that we could just join in made a lot of sense. Obviously, the one-team concept only goes so far. We're competitors. But we're also teammates." As his chief engineer, Todd Holbert, puts it: "For the first three months, all of us [Davis, Petty and Evernham] were working in the same building—the R&D facility Petty built especially for the program."

Davis already had drivers Ward Burton and Dave Blaney under contract. A spacious new shop gave the team plenty of room to develop the Dodge. Terry Elledge headed up the engine program while the team's R&D duo—Holbert and fabricator Dave Nelson—went to work on new chassis and body templates.

So, as the 2000 season opened, the Dodge program appeared to be set with three teams and seven cars. But

Although each of the five Dodge Winston Cup teams has its own R&D staff, factory engineers are the backbone of the Intrepid R/T development program.

JUNE 2000

Andy Graves, general manager of Chip Ganassi Racing with Felix Sabates, starts working on the Dodge Cup program at the Team SABCO shop in Mooresville, North Carolina.

▼ JUNE 2000

Melling Racing officially becomes the fourth Dodge team for 2001. Stacy Compton, who had driven a Dodge in the Craftsman Truck Series in 1999, will be the driver.

JUNE 2000

The Dodge Cup engine gets its first on-track test at Kentucky Speedway. Besides Compton, Elliott, Atwood, and Petty, Dodge Craftsman Truck Series drivers Dennis Setzer and Steve Grissom get seat time.

▲ JULY 2000

Ernie Elliott signs a deal to build Dodge Cup engines for Chip Ganassi.

at Daytona, Evernham—who was covering the truck race for ESPN—happened to visit with another Hendrick alumnus, Andy Graves. Graves had recently hired on with four-time CART championship owner Chip Ganassi to build a Cup team, but they hadn't yet signed with a manufacturer. "If the day comes when Chip wants to move forward with Dodge," Evernham told Graves, "let me know."

A swing-for-the-fences businessman fond of gambling on high-risk propositions, Ganassi quickly recognized the benefits of hooking up with a newcomer. "The road for me coming into Winston Cup was fraught with land mines," Ganassi explains. "For example, I had to be realistic and accept the fact that I wasn't going to be at the top of the food chain with GM and Ford."

Looking for a more favorable deal, Ganassi met with Dodge officials. They were reluctant for several reasons. First, Ganassi was new to NASCAR. Second, and more to the point, Dodge had budgeted for only three teams. But

Julow hadn't factored in the force of Ganassi's personality and the clarity of his vision. "After about thirty minutes," Julow recalls, "I said, 'We need to go racing with this guy.'"

On Sunday, May 30, Graves oversaw the Ganassi effort that saw Juan Montoya dominate the Indianapolis 500. The following Tuesday, Graves went to work on the Dodge program in the Team SABCO shop in Mooresville, North Carolina, which Ganassi had just bought from Felix Sabates. Graves freed up space by clearing out Sabates' Busch operation, then outfitted the temporary shop with new set-up plates and fabrication equipment. About fifteen people were hired and placed under the direction of Ray Hall, who'd moved with Graves from Hendrick to Ganassi.

Unlike Sabates, Graves wanted the team to hang its own bodies. "Aerodynamics is so important these days," he says. On the other hand, he chose to farm out the engine program to Ernie Elliott, best known for his work with Ford and his brother Bill Elliott. "I liked the idea of getting in on

Dodge's one-team concept is based on the notion that two heads—or, in the case of the Winston Cup program, five teams—are better than one. Here's a perfect illustration of the concept in action, as members of the Petty, Melling, and Ganassi teams pore over data and share insights during a test session.

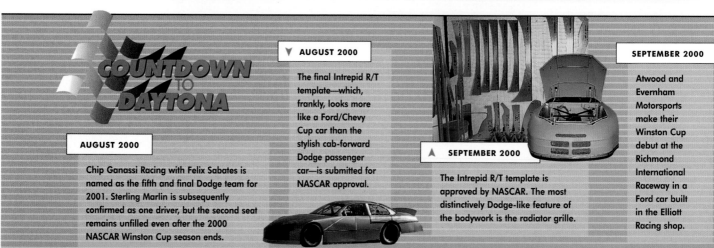

COUNTDOWN TO DAYTONA

AUGUST 2000

Chip Ganassi Racing with Felix Sabates is named as the fifth and final Dodge team for 2001. Sterling Marlin is subsequently confirmed as one driver, but the second seat remains unfilled even after the 2000 NASCAR Winston Cup season ends.

▼ AUGUST 2000

The final Intrepid R/T template—which, frankly, looks more like a Ford/Chevy Cup car than the stylish cab-forward Dodge passenger car—is submitted for NASCAR approval.

▲ SEPTEMBER 2000

The Intrepid R/T template is approved by NASCAR. The most distinctively Dodge-like feature of the bodywork is the radiator grille.

SEPTEMBER 2000

Atwood and Evernham Motorsports make their Winston Cup debut at the Richmond International Raceway in a Ford car built in the Elliott Racing shop.

the ground floor with Dodge," Ernie says. "Obviously, the ground floor with GM and Ford was a long time ago."

Team SABCO driver Sterling Marlin will stay on to drive one of the Ganassi cars. The second seat remained unfilled even after the 2000 Cup season ended. Meanwhile, and completely unexpectedly, Dodge was still negotiating with a fifth team, Melling Racing. A one-car team that had fallen on hard times since its glory days with Bill Elliott, Melling didn't seem to fit the Dodge profile. But there were two points arguing in its favor. First, driver Stacy Compton had scored a record six poles in a Dodge truck the previous year. Second, owner Mark Melling had dealt with Dodge during the negotiations that ended up with Bill Elliott getting to use the #9 he'd made famous (with Melling Racing) during the Eighties.

By the spring of 1999, Melling was ready to buddy up with Dodge. "It was a no-brainer for us, especially since we're a one-car team," says business manager Lake Speed, Jr. And since Melling didn't have the resources to develop the 2001 Dodge while continuing to race a Ford in 2000, the one-team concept was a lifesaver. "We're trusting the other teams to share their knowledge and know-how," Speed says. And sometimes more than knowledge and know-how: When Melling needed a new crew chief, he picked up Chad Knaus from Evernham Motorsports. And Ernie Elliott will build his engines.

So Dodge will have five teams and ten cars contesting the Winston Cup championship this year. The engine is the biggest question mark. But the Ronnie Hopkins chassis all the cars will be built around are proven winners. And while early tests suggested that the bodies were a bit draggy, they should be good in race trim.

"If we come out of the box halfway competitive, I think we might win a race before the end of the year," Richard Petty says. "But I'm not making any predictions. I don't believe in predictions. We know what we ought to do. We've just got to go out and do it." ∎

Dodge will have five teams and ten cars contesting the Winston Cup championship this year. The engine is the biggest question mark. But the chassis all the cars will be built around are proven winners.

All for one and one for all—until race day, that is. Todd Holbert (above center), chief engineer at Bill Davis Racing, confers with members of the Petty crew. Left: Ganassi's Andy Graves and Melling's Chad Knaus and Stacy Compton.

SEPTEMBER 2000

Dodge engine parts are presented to NASCAR. They bear no relationship to the motors that have been raced successfully in the Craftsman Truck Series.

OCTOBER 2000

Young Busch Series veteran Buckshot Jones is named to fill the Petty Enterprises seat vacated by the fatal crash of Adam Petty.

OCTOBER 2000

Dodge holds its first official manufacturer's test at Talladega Superspeedway. This also marks the Intrepid R/T Winston Cup car's first superspeedway outing.

NOVEMBER 2000

NASCAR approves the Dodge Cup engine.

FEBRUARY 2001

2001 Daytona 500. The countdown ends.

WIN ON SUNDAY, SELL ON MONDAY

By William Neely

PHOTOGRAPHY BY DON HUNTER

When you come right down to it, there were only two parts to the early days of NASCAR racing. Or so the old-timers say. Part One: There was a lot of slamming and banging, dusty slamming and banging. You see, dust was one of the requisites. Part Two: There was a passel of battleship-sized Hudson Hornets roaring around the primitive dirt tracks; the red clouds came from the rooster tails of powdery clay spewing from behind their wheels. Week after week they chased each other toward a checkered flag and a hurrying sunset.

Other cars won races, but nobody seems to remember. Or maybe even care. They loved the Hudsons because, well, you didn't see too many of them on the streets in those days. The track was a different story; the fans wondered if anybody would ever tame the Twin-H Power Hornets. Case in point: Hudson won twenty-seven of the thirty-one races in 1952.

There's little doubt that racing kept the Hudson Motor Car Company in business for two or three years longer than fate was ominously and impatiently trying to decree. It was the first time auto manufacturers took racing seriously as a sales tool. Racing did for Hudson what decades of marketing pitches had failed to do—sell cars. Of course, it opened eyes in a few corporate board rooms, too.

Once in a while an Olds 88 or a flathead Ford or a Lincoln challenged the "step-down-ride" Hudsons; anything else might just as well have been put back on the trailer. Assuming, of course, they had a trailer.

The monopoly lasted from 1949 until 1953, and then racing's most exclusive fraternity—the winner's circle—took on another member. Suddenly there was an extra force with which to be reckoned—the adroit Dodge of Lee Petty.

Petty was the first to win a NASCAR race in a Dodge. He opened the 1953 season at West Palm Beach, driving a Diplomat coupe, and wound up winning the race two laps ahead of the second-place car of Jimmy Lewallen. Petty unwittingly created a niche for Dodge in NASCAR racing. In 1977, Neil Bonnett won the last race in a Dodge at Ontario. What happened in between is something Mopar racing fans will never forget. Nor should, for that matter. What put them out of racing still puzzles most fans.

Lee Petty beat the Hudsons five times in 1953 with his Red Ram Hemi V-8; Jimmy Paschal added another in his nimble Dodge. Two years later, the Hornets were relegated to museums and used-car lots as Dodge struggled toward the top.

An all-out factory Dodge effort didn't come along until the mid-Sixties, though. As it turned out, the ardor to sell passenger cars—the same thing that had kept Hudson alive a tad longer—brought Dodge into racing. In a big way. But not with a whimper like the Fifties; this time it was with a roar—a fervent, where-the-rubber-meets-the-road warfare.

The new decade was just beginning, but already the nation had begun to turn its collective eyes to stock car tracks throughout the country. That got some attention in Detroit. Frank Wylie, who was soon to be named the top Dodge racing guy, had become more and more intrigued with the success of racing-newcomer Pontiac on the oval tracks of the Southeast. So he decided to drive on down there from Detroit and see for himself.

"I drove all through the Carolinas," says Wylie, "and it was just what I expected: There was a white Pontiac sitting in every damn driveway. I knew it was time to get [Dodge] involved."

And get involved they did. In 1964 Dodge won fourteen races, with legendary drivers such as David Pearson, Junior Johnson, A. J. Foyt, and Buck Baker behind the wheel. That's involvement.

As you might imagine, Dodge passenger cars began to grace southern driveways. "Win on Sunday, sell on Monday" became the credo of car manufacturers. This time Dodge was a beneficiary.

The trip to the top took far more than luck. It required about as much planning as a moon shot, and if they had been running that, David Pearson probably would have driven that one, too.

The first task that faced the Mopar engineers was to streamline the bodies. And then they dug around and came up with some blueprints and set out to build the engine that would make their cars run like scalded dogs. It was called the Hemi.

Right: Maurice Petty, brother Richard's engine man, and Bill Gazaway, NASCAR tech czar, examine carburetor restrictor plates, mandated by the sanctioning body in an attempt to slow down the Hemi-powered Mopars. Facing page: Two of the most successful car-builders of the Sixties and Seventies, Ray Fox, top right, and Cotton Owens, bottom. Their cars were no strangers to Victory Lane.

Next they added a trick from the racing program of the early Fifties. The engine had a hemispherical combustion chamber with double rocker shafts. The huge intake and exhaust valves were placed on opposite sides of the combustion chamber, rather than side by side, giving the engine a free-breathing chamber. The spark plug sat right in the center of the combustion chamber for efficient ignition. Just as it had in the early Fifties for Lee Petty, the combination produced incredible power at the top end.

To test the whole package, they went to Goodyear's five-mile circular test track in San Angelo, Texas, with their 426 Hemi-engined cars and turned the unbelievable speeds of more than 180 miles per hour. They were rocket ships for the time.

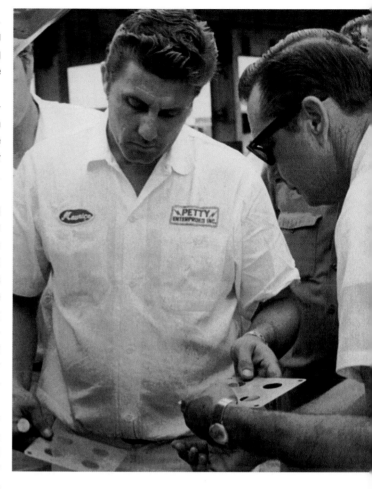

The Hemi-powered Dodges were still under wraps when Dan Gurney won the 1964 race at Riverside in a Ford, but when the Mopar teams unloaded their cars at Daytona there was one noticeable difference: Painted on the hoods were the words "Hemi-Powered." The Ford, Chevy, and Pontiac teams weren't sure what it really meant, but they had a feeling they were about to find out.

They didn't have to scratch their heads for long. Paul Goldsmith qualified one of the Hemis at 174.910 miles per hour, which was good enough for the pole (at a whopping ten miles per hour faster than the year before). Richard Petty was right behind him in another Mopar at 174.418. The Fords qualified in the 160s, which, all of a sudden, was lumbering. You have to keep in mind that tires and other equipment in general, not to mention technology, was in a Paleolithic age.

When Junior Johnson won the first Daytona qualifying race in a Ray Fox–prepared Dodge and Bobby Isaac won the second qualifier in a Ray Nichels Dodge, Ford began to see the writing on the wall.

During the 1963 season, Ford had adopted the slogan "Total Performance" for its racing endeavors. They continued the campaign for 1964. After Mopar drivers Petty, Jimmy Pardue, and Goldsmith crossed the finish line one-two-three in the Daytona 500, Chrysler PR man Dick Williford went through the pits passing out badges that read simply "Total What?"

To continue the superiority, A. J. Foyt won the Firecracker 400 later that year in a Nichels Dodge, followed by five other Hemis. When Buck Baker took his Dodge to the checkered flag at the celebrated Southern 500 at Darlington, the racing world was convinced that this was no fluke. The Hemis ruled the stock car world.

The domination continued all season, and Petty ended up winning the championship in 1964 by a colossal margin. In fact, the entire season was so big for Mopar that it was to cost them their beloved engine. In an effort to slow things down a bit, NASCAR banned the Hemi engine for 1965, citing "safety" as the reason. Also a new wheelbase ruling dictated that Dodge would have to run their

Air Lift, A Family Affair
By William Neely

Racing fans have learned to accept high-tech everything. No problem. Computers are commonplace on pit road; engineers abound. Fans keep up with their favorite drivers with elaborate listening devices; during the race they tune in to the same radio conversations as their heroes. The whole thing is Captain Kirk with corporate logos. There's sophisticated technology everywhere you look.

But there was a time when a device as simple as a rubber air bladder was about as refined as it got when it came to race-car suspension. Add to that simplified device the fact that it was delivered with the family car (no speedy, overnight express service: a station wagon, right to the garage area) and you've got the good ol' days of NASCAR racing. It was a family sort of affair. No fanfare, no television cameras. Family.

Keep in mind that stock cars were—well, I don't know exactly how to tell you this—stock. So these bladders were a big thing. They were called Air Lift, and a lot of races were won because of them. Racing was a far less opulent society, so it was imperative that budgets be kept down. It made a lot of sense if the various teams didn't have to lug around a passel of extra springs, among other things, to be used in case the cars needed more heft in the corners.

The Air Lift bags were inserted in the middle of the coil springs and inflated; the more air added to them, the stronger they became. Simple.

NASCAR's legendary car-builder Smokey Yunick recalls the Air Lift days in the most basic terms: "They were helper springs that you put inside the coils to run the spring rate up. If you got too much air in them you could just let some out. We didn't have the technology to know exactly how much to put in or take out; it was just trial and error. But it was a whole lot quicker than having to change springs half a dozen times. With one set of springs and a set of Air Lifts, we could dial it in.

"The Air Lift company was out of Michigan, and the whole family came to the races. I mean, they were all related. They even had a sign painter to letter 'Air Lift' on the front fenders of the race cars. They didn't even have decals.

"They were real nice people. Why, if we needed something lettered on our race cars, we'd wait til we got to the track and go to Archie, their sign painter; he'd take care of us. They were part of us," Smokey says.

Air Lift was primarily a product for passenger cars and pickup trucks, but NASCAR gave them the sales boost they needed to sell their product to the public. In the late Fifties, they toured the whole country with an Oldsmobile Eighty Eight demonstrator car. They pumped up the right front air bag until it was super strong, so they were able to take off the left front wheel and drive all over the place on three wheels. "I'll tell you one thing," Smokey says, "it made people stop and look."

Ray Fox, whose Dodge race cars were among the most successful in NASCAR in the Sixties, remembers Air Lift: "They made it possible for a lot of teams to win races, teams that didn't have the money to haul around a lot of extra parts. I guess most of the guys stopped using Air Lifts when somebody came up with the rubber wedges that they inserted in the springs. They were a lot faster to use during a race; you just reached in and pulled them out or pounded them in, as opposed to actually letting out or putting in air," he says.

NASCAR allowed the use of Air Lifts from 1960 to 1962. Today, the Lansing, Michigan–based company makes a range of load-leveling air springs for pickups, cars, and motorhomes, as well as a line of lowering kits for street rods.

big Polara. "The Polara was designed strictly as a luxury automobile," said Ronney Householder, director of competition for Chrysler. "They're big, with a lot of gadgets and fancy stuff. Weight distribution on these cars was meant for highway comfort, not racing."

"Racing has always prided itself on being progressive," said Chrysler's Bob Anderson. "Here we are backing up." And then they walked out.

With the quickness of, say, a Hemi, Chrysler was out of NASCAR. So, too, was Richard Petty who, left without a ride, went drag racing with his Hemi-powered race car, appropriately named "Outlawed."

By mid-season 1965, with the crowds down considerably at NASCAR races because of the Chrysler boycott, Bill France made an unprecedented decision; he reinstated the Hemi engine for tracks of one mile or less and for road courses. The Hemis came back. So, too, did the crowds. They had wanted competition, not just a Ford parade.

Richard Petty set a record in 1967, which surely will never be broken. He became "King Richard" when he won twenty-seven races in his trademark blue Number 43 race car. The new monarch won twenty-one races the following year.

Each year seemed to be better than the one before for Dodge. Record after record fell. In 1969 at Talladega, Buddy Baker became the first driver to exceed 200 miles per hour on a closed circuit—in a winged Dodge Charger Daytona.

Thanks to years of Superbirds and Charger Daytonas, Mopar continued to thrill NASCAR fans. Between the years of 1974 and 1977, Richard Petty and his faithful Dodge Charger won thirty-one of the 120 races and two NASCAR

Each year seemed to be better than the one before for Dodge. Record after record fell.

championships. Still, there were measures taken in an attempt to "slow them down."

All of the squabbling with the ruling body took its toll. Chrysler, slowly becoming disenchanted, put less and less into the racing program; they felt that the other companies were given too many advantages. By 1978, Ford and Chevrolet were allowed to race smaller Thunderbirds, Cougars, and Monte Carlos, yet Dodge was not permitted to run their smaller Diplomat. This left Chrysler holding the bag, with only the bulky Dodge Magnum, which their two top drivers, Richard Petty and Neil Bonnett, as hard as they tried, could not make competitive.

"Dodge did as much to boost NASCAR as the other way around," says racing's resident guru, H. A. (Humpy) Wheeler, president of Speedway Mortorsports. "In 1964, when the rear-engine invasion hit Indianapolis, they [Indy]

had a commanding lead as the number one series. NASCAR's problem was that General Motors had hit the road. It was all Ford. But Dodge's commitment and the exploits of Richard Petty began the swing, and by the Seventies, NASCAR had taken over the top spot in auto racing throughout the world.

"There was one major element that did it," says Wheeler, "the magnificent Hemi engine. It had everything drivers wanted—torque, dependability, and tremendous power. And all of this was against some very formidable Ford engines, most notably the 428. Ford had put a lot of money in the engine program."

Assuredly the Hemi was a dominant factor in Dodge's tremendous success, but that wasn't all. Outstanding engineering contributed greatly. Some of it came in the form of Larry Rathgeb, one of the Chrysler chassis

Two of NASCAR's top mechanics, Buddy Parrott, left, and Harry Hyde, work at getting tires ready for the Dodge Daytona, using what was a state-of-the-art tire balancer for the time. The K & K–sponsored race car awaits the attack at a class record on the Bonneville Salt Flats in Utah.

Dodge looks to return to its glory days in NASCAR, when Richard Petty became the King of stock car racing and it wasn't unusual to see a couple of Dodges leading the way.

Dodge's entry into NASCAR Winston Cup competition for the 2001 season promises to be anything but ordinary. In fact, it's very different.

experts. He was light years ahead of anybody else on chassis in those days; so far that most of the proclaimed experts, stalwarts such as Junior Johnson, Bud Moore, and Leonard Wood, didn't pay much attention when Rathgeb told them they needed more left-side weight. His total insistence on this entirely new approach was a major reason for the success of the Hemi race cars, because Dodge was the first to adapt this theory. Nobody else agreed. Superspeedway racing was still a learning experience. Left-side weight is so primary today that it's hard to imagine anything else.

Not only did the Dodges run well, they were distinctive. They looked good, which Wylie thought was important. "Please the fans," was his goal. If you can do it from the winner's circle, so much the better.

He enlisted the aid of Lippincott and Margolis, a New York graphics firm, to come up with car colors and paint schemes for the Dodges. The Day-Glo colors looked sensational; in fact, they livened up the whole entertainment spectacle.

Now racing is about to go through the exercise once again: The "new kid on the block" syndrome. Dodge's entry

It was the early 1970s and Dodge was riding high on the high banks at Daytona (far left). Dodge will be back again in the 2001 Daytona 500, with cars such as the Evernham Motorsports No. 19 Intrepid R/T (right). Ray Evernham (at left) and drivers Casey Atwood (center) and Bill Elliott show the car during the 2000 season.

into NASCAR Winston Cup competition for the 2001 season promises to be anything but ordinary. In fact, it's very different. According to the guys at Auburn Hills, Michigan, and Stuttgart, Germany, it's "Dodge Different," which is a central theme in all Dodge advertising. Wonder if they've enlisted the services of Lippincott and Margolis again?

They're coming back with the same apparent agonizing thoroughness. They've hired Ray Evernham, the crew chief who led Jeff Gordon to three Winston Cup championships, to establish the program. And, after a year and a half of preparation, NASCAR has approved the body templates for the wind-tunnel slick Dodge Intrepid R/T race car. The gloves are off.

"Working with the Dodge people to bring them back to Winston Cup is a once-in-a-lifetime opportunity," says Evernham. "Like the people at Dodge, I'm committed to winning." In the words of Keith Jackson: "Whoa, Nelly."

According to Lou Patane, vice-president of motorsports and Mopar Performance Parts, "We intend to be competitive consistently from the beginning. There is no point in starting if you don't plan to finish."

So, fasten your seat belts, Sally, it's 1964 again. ∎

DODGING THE RULES

How Dodge's Intrepid R/T Winston Cup car was made unique in spite of NASCAR's hefty rulebook. By Eddie Alterman

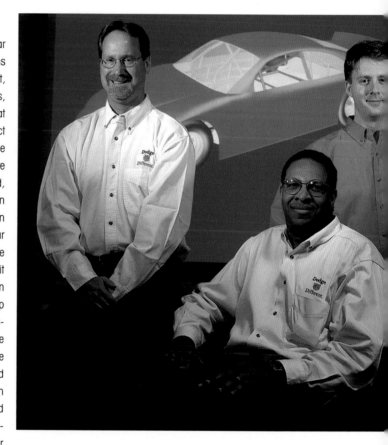

It is a misconception in stock-car racing that the engine is what wins races. This arises from the fact that, unlike NASCAR bodies and chassis, the engine is the only component that is custom built and not designed to the strict formulas governing the rest of the car. While it is indeed true that all NASCAR bodies are built to a template and that every tube, weld, and suspension component is stipulated in NASCAR's 300-page rulebook, the way in which the teams tailor these ready-to-wear pieces can be as important as ultimate horsepower—especially in races that limit engine output with air-restrictor plates. In reality, the amount of work done to set up and fine tune a car's aerodynamic and suspension packages would shock even the most overworked Boeing engineer. These efforts are both staggering in breadth and minuscule in scope; no part of a Winston Cup car's body or chassis escapes the cold stare of analysis, but neither is any part conspicuously changed. When you consider that in many Winston Cup races, only four-tenths of a second separates the first car from the last, it seems clear that the unseen details are what really claim the checkered flag. Perhaps no manufacturer in Winston Cup has embraced this concept as strongly as Dodge, and no other carmaker uses as much technology as Dodge to pursue those tiny parts of a second.

Dodge has a distinct advantage over other Winston Cup teams: Its effort is backed by a 12,000-strong engineering corps that can be marshalled to the front of Dodge's Cup battle. Race central is housed in the DaimlerChrysler Technical Center in Auburn Hills, and although the core of the racing team is small at twelve men, DaimlerChrysler has made it clear to these men and their team-owning col-leagues in North Carolina that the entire Tech Center engineering staff is at their disposal.

So even if the Tech Center is far removed from the garages of the Carolinas, it is linked to the South via T1 lines, common software programs, and an intense focus on winning. The vision of the Intrepid R/T on the Winston Cup podium looms over this place. As we sat with the Dodge Racing team in a briefing room within the Tech Center, it became clear that, although the weather might be cooler in the suburbs of Detroit, there is as much heat in this building as there is in the whole of Charlotte.

The methodology that produces this kind of intensity is a familiar one. In fact, it's the same as DaimlerChrysler uses in producing its fast-to-market passenger cars. It goes like

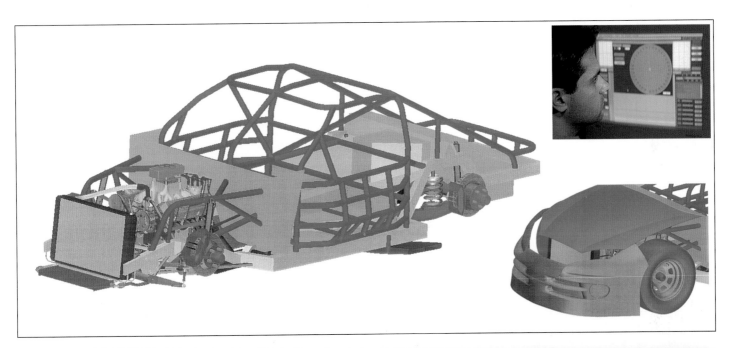

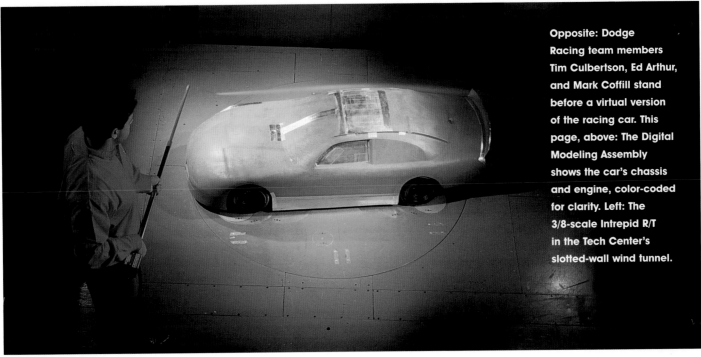

Opposite: Dodge
Racing team members
Tim Culbertson, Ed Arthur,
and Mark Coffill stand
before a virtual version
of the racing car. This
page, above: The Digital
Modeling Assembly
shows the car's chassis
and engine, color-coded
for clarity. Left: The
3/8-scale Intrepid R/T
in the Tech Center's
slotted-wall wind tunnel.

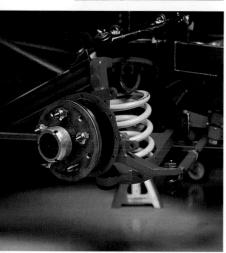

this: Everyone works on the same thing at the same time. No papers are passed from office to office, no one has to shuffle pulp through a three-part approval process, and no one has to wait while the proposal sits on someone's desk. The design and modification of the Dodge Intrepid racing car is a symphonic undertaking. It involves World HQ, team garages, and NASCAR officials, and it is a slippery process, precluding a classical, linear timeline.

If the genesis of the Intrepid R/T body and chassis is a symphony, with players entering and exiting at the appropriate moments, the conductor who brings it all together is Tim Culbertson, Dodge NASCAR Winston Cup program manager and Winston Cup chassis lead. For reasons peculiar to both Dodge's design systems and NASCAR's myriad parts prescriptions, Culbertson didn't give us a who-did-what-when account of the build-up, but he ably explained, almost a year after the project was initiated, all the fine tuning done to the Intrepid R/T's chassis and body. As we sat together

before a large overhead projector loaded with Microsoft PowerPoint presentations, Culbertson introduced me to the car's chassis men and its aerodynamicists, in the process stating the overarching philosophy that guided the Intrepid R/T through its birth.

"We are working for the racing teams, not the other way around. Our job is to use all our production-car resources here to meet requirements down in Charlotte. Our changes might seem minute, but it's the little things that make you successful in racing. If our changes are good for a thousandth of a second over the other guys, hey, I'll take that."

In optimizing the car's chassis, Culbertson recognized a few areas for continuous improvement. These include controlling overall stiffness, standardizing build quality, and understanding the dynamics of those pieces common to all Cup cars, such as the Detroit Locker limited-slip rear axle and the steering system—items traditionally slapped on the car unexamined. With regard to the tube-frame chassis,

In the garage. Top: The Intrepid R/T's front suspension in the paint shop. Above: The Evernham team's assembled front suspension. Right: Some finishing touches are put on the Ronnie Hopkins chassis in the Petty garage.

Culbertson says: "The frame is like a spring itself, and we have to know how to best tune it for short tracks, road courses, or superspeedways. The pickup points for the suspension may move around, or we can cut parts of the chassis off to make it stiffer, or we can change the gauges of the bars themselves."

The tool that allows the frame to be thus modified is called DMA, or Digital Modeling Assembly. DMA generates a dimensionally accurate image of the car that all members of both the engineering team in Auburn Hills and the racing teams in North Carolina can access and change in real time. The cars are then updated with the changes every night. Brad Smith, the engineer running the DMA demonstration, put up a color-coded computer model of the car on the screen and asked us to call out a change that he would execute. We told him to move the left front damper forward eleven millimeters, and with a couple of taps, the gray strut popped into its new position. He then took the virtual tire off

and enlarged the modified suspension, in order to show us that our change introduced a clearance conflict—the gray damper was now in the path of the green brake disc.

But if all goes well, DMA can send successful design changes to a lab in the Tech Center's basement, which will then rapid-prototype a part. Using stereo lithography, a 3-D printer of sorts cuts a manifold, or a brake disc, or a trailing arm out of plastic and wood. These parts are subsequently tested. With the push of a button, engineers can send the part's design to engineers who will determine how air flows around it. And to get an idea of how the new piece works on the car itself, Dodge uses the Tech Center's Synthesis of Simulation Technology (SST), that predicts how a component will function on a virtual Intrepid.

Chrysler's first application of SST came on its 1993 LH sedans. For those incredulous souls who wondered how Chrysler could turn its LH show cars into road cars in 30 months, SST is telling. The simulator replicates chassis,

Left: Ray Hall of Ganassi preps an R/T for its engine. Below: The Petty team's Todd Privett assembles the jewel-like transmission, which is polished on every surface to eliminate stress points and edges.

If Dodge Racing can better understand the kinematics of the steering gear, or the Detroit Locker axle, or the tire's contact patches, it can peer into those parts of the car that most teams consider black art.

aerodynamic, engine, tire, and environmental behaviors, in the process saving countless days of real-world testing. In chassis simulations, SST employs Finite Element Analysis (to evaluate the flexing characteristics of a part) and Suspension Kinematics Modeling (to predict how said part will move). SST is supplemented with and informed by real-world exams using data acquisition equipment, to make sure the tests in the simulator conform to the car's on-track behavior. SST is therefore useful for parts the Dodge team makes themselves, but it is even more important for those components that all teams use. If Dodge Racing can better understand the kinematics of the steering gear, or the Detroit

Locker axle, or the tire's contact patches, it can peer into those parts of the car that most teams consider black art.

On the subject of black arts, none are blacker or more artsy than racing car aerodynamics, and here, Jeff Bordner enters the picture. Bordner is Dodge's senior NASCAR Winston Cup aerodynamic development engineer, and he is charged with the fabrication, research, and testing of the Intrepid's body. Well, actually, three bodies: Bordner's team must tailor shapes for the high-downforce requirements of short tracks, the intermediate requirements of intermediate courses, and the low-drag requirements of super-speedways. These designs must also address thermal

Clockwise: Body templates on a rack; an English wheel shapes part of the body; identical plastic noses and tails are the only body parts that Dodge Winston Cup teams share.

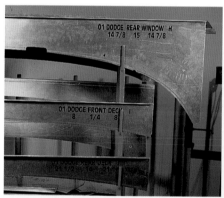

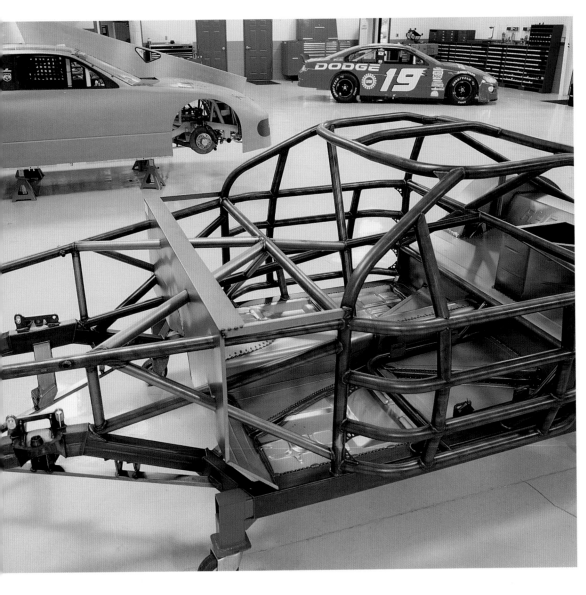

A sneak peek into one of the hottest garages in Charlotte, the Evernham workshop. In the foreground is the R/T chassis, gauged and bent to the team's specifications. Behind it, on jack stands, is the primered body over a working chassis. The Intrepid R/T show car, introduced at the 2000 North American International Auto Show, is parked in front of Ray Evernham's copious tool stash.

concerns like brake cooling and directing heat away from the driver.

NASCAR specifies twenty-five templates for each body structure, little metal ribs to which the car's body must conform. There are templates for the nose, the hood, the A-, B-, and C-pillars, the windshield, the doors, the taillights, all spoilers, and the overall silhouette. Within these templates are three different tolerances that Winston Cup teams can manipulate. Bordner lets the Dodge teams in Charlotte adjust the tolerances, and works instead on making the primary body as good as it can be, aerodynamically speaking. This, he says, fits with Dodge's "one team" approach: "We want to get all the teams the best possible hardware, and let the Dodge team that's made the best adjustments to the chassis and body win the race."

The body program began in the wind tunnel, in the basement of the Tech Center, in late 1999. We followed the team from the briefing room down to the aero lab, which houses a small, 3/8-scale wind tunnel of semi-open jet design, which means it has walls to break up its wrathful, particle-accelerating tunnel of air. (DaimlerChrysler is currently building a new, full scale, open-jet wind tunnel on the Tech Center grounds, to the tune of $50 million.) The downsized wind machine is capable of replicating speeds of 180 mph from 1200 bhp of fan turbine power. The cars that are tested here are 3/8-scale themselves, so-called Advanced Models with carbon bodies and driver compartments. These models sit on a cylinder scale embedded in the floor, and the car's tires are set into pins on the scale that are able to measure downforce.

In optimizing the car's chassis, Culbertson recognized
a few areas for continuous improvement. These included
controlling overall stiffness, standardizing build quality, and
understanding the dynamics of those pieces common
to all Cup cars—items that traditionally have
been slapped on the car unexamined.

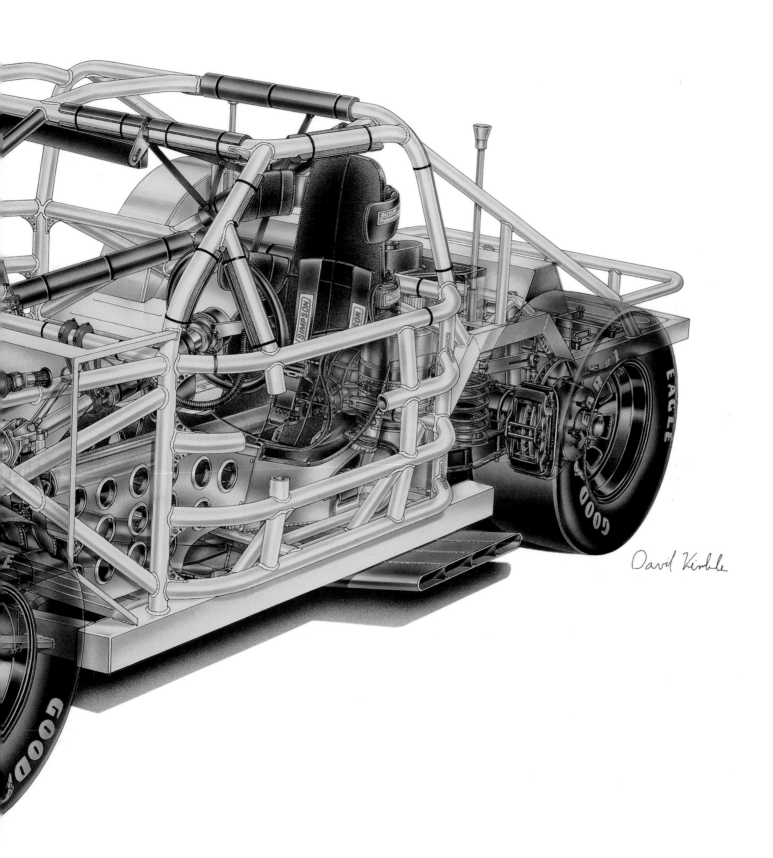

David Kimble

In 2001 Bill Elliott will once again be in a red #9—the number came courtesy of Melling Racing—and Elliott Racing will merge with Evernham Motorsports. Says Elliott, "This gives us the opportunity to make a fresh start with a very high-profile program that all eyes in the racing world will be watching."

But with all the body's invisible airflow surfaces, the wind tunnel only provides the broadest outline of the car's aerodynamic picture. After it comes out of the wind tunnel, the body is shaped by its own set of computer-based tools distinct from those used on the chassis. In forming the body, the airmeisters call upon Wake Imaging technology and Computational Fluid Dynamics, both of which sound a lot more mysterious than they actually are.

Wake Imaging, a system developed with the help of

Boeing, simply allows engineers to see a colorized picture of the air as it flows over the car. Air pressure corresponds to the colors of the visible spectrum, with low-pressure areas rendered in red, high-pressure zones in blue. If the wake imager indicates that there is too much unwanted pressure—i.e., drag—around the body, or if it reports that the more forceful air isn't going where it needs to go, the team will modify its shape.

Computational Fluid Dynamics does essentially the same

Clockwise from above: Fiberglass panel pop-riveted into the steel body shows the tolerances of the hood gaps; the R/T's instument panel, steering wheel removed; closing the intake for high-speed testing; aero flap; tape indicates the position of the aero hump for superspeedways.

thing, but allows the engineers to see how both air and fluids flow inside the car, from the radiator and the intake manifold to the fuel system. The team says they've spent a surprising amount of time crafting the intake manifold, to provide even breathing to each cylinder in the battle for endurance and power efficiency. Perhaps the best part about CFD is that it allows you to simulate events you wouldn't normally be able to in a wind tunnel. For example, CFD can mimic the swath two cars drafting at 190 mph cut through the air. And it can tell you what those cars will look like drafting next to a wall. A wind tunnel also cannot simulate a rolling ground surface, nor a 100-degree race day, nor can it tell you how the driver is holding up inside the car.

The results of Dodge's aerodynamicists' work has been creative, to say the least. All the virtual information compiled in the aero lab has led to very tangible things like the large bubble in the cars' hoods. This protrusion forces the air onto the top third of the windshield, expanding the low-pressure bubble that feeds the carburetor through the cowl vent. Even more interesting is the way the computers formed the rear of the body—specifically, the transitional corners where the C-pillar meets the rear deck lid. Knowing, through CFD, that more air hits the rear spoiler from those

corners than from the roof, Dodge has designed three different pillars and rear quarter panels for the three body shapes. For a superspeedway, they insert a dowager's hump into the C-pillar and the body side, which raises airflow enough to clear the top edge of the spoiler. The intermediate-track body has a smaller, rounder C-pillar with a soft intersection with the side and deck. Finally, the short-track car's C-pillar looks fairly stock, with a sharp angle where the pillar, the quarter panel, and the rear deck meet. This directs the air coming around the corner to the full width of the rear spoiler's base.

The team presented these bodies for approval to NASCAR in late summer. NASCAR approved them in August. At the end of September, though, NASCAR added a two-inch high strip to all Cup cars that runs across the roof, right where a taxi sign would go. The sanctioning body has also added a 3/4-inch Gurney flap to the top edge of the spoiler. Bordner says the teams hate these modifications because of how significantly they slow the cars down. NASCAR, it seems, has thrown its constituents another curveball, but the teams are used to this. So it's back to the wind tunnel and back to the computers for more chasing of milliseconds. ∎

The Melling Team's No. 92 Kodiak Intrepid undergoes track testing.

BIG NUMBERS

Bigger numbers than Big Bill ever dreamed.   By Joe Schulte

"Nothing stands still in this world and we don't know how big stock car racing can be if it's handled properly." Those could be the words of a NASCAR executive in 2001 as he pitches the sanctioning body's marketing potential to a group of media barons or a conference room full of financial analysts. In reality, those were the words of William Henry Getty France, spoken over fifty-three years ago, as he sought support for his fledgling sanctioning body from a group of stock car racing enthusiasts. "Big Bill" was convinced that the sport of stock car racing could grow if there was a national organization to create and enforce a set of fair and consistent rules to govern the cars and competitors. It was from this basic belief that NASCAR was born and from which it draws its success today.

Evidence would certainly suggest that Mr. France knew what he was talking about. As racing enters the new millennium, NASCAR's Winston Cup Series stands head and shoulders above all other forms of motorsport in America. When it comes to spectators and sponsorships, some very big numbers define its success.

For starters, NASCAR now has a TV rights package involving NBC, TBS, and Fox (Fox Sports and FX) that is bigger than the NBA, bigger than the NHL, and bigger than the PGA; $2.8 billion dollars over the length of the agreement. This should come as no surprise when you consider: Winston Cup average cable network ratings triple those of Major League Baseball, the National Basketball Association, or the National Hockey League. When it comes to Nielsen TV ratings for sports on broadcast networks, NASCAR Winston Cup trails only the National Football League.

While no numbers are being discussed, the recently inked deal between NASCAR and Turner Sports might wind up bigger than any sports property has yet seen from the Internet. Specifically, Turner has acquired NASCAR's Internet rights and will become producer of NASCAR.com, the official Web site of NASCAR.

What makes this scenario interesting are the shared interests of Turner Sports (who will split the second half of NASCAR's 2001 season with NBC television) and AOL, both owned by Time-Warner. Can everybody spell media convergence?

The agreement gives Turner the ability to create online promotions and enhanced broadcasts/Webcasts for all televised NASCAR events that will deliver a level of viewer involvement unique in sports.

In terms of attendance numbers, the NASCAR Winston Cup Series is in a league by itself, attracting an estimated 6.5 million fans to its thirty-four events in 1999—an average of over 191,000-paying customers per event. To put that in perspective, the average NASCAR Winston Cup race weekend will draw nearly three times as many fans as the NFL did for this year's Super Bowl.

It also is apparent that NASCAR fan interest in stock car racing doesn't end when the checkered flag falls. Sales of NASCAR licensed goods, from die-cast collectible model cars to apparel, are estimated to have reached $1.2 billion dollars last year. A very big number, once again outstripping every other pro sport in the land, with the exception of the NFL.

WINSTON CUP ATTENDANCE

Year	Number of races*	Number of tracks	Attendance
1990	29	16	3.3 million
1991	29	16	3.5 million
1992	29	16	3.7 million
1993	30	17	4.0 million
1994	31	18	4.9 million
1995	31	18	5.3 million
1996	31	18	5.6 million
1997	32	20	6.1 million
1998	33	20	6.3 million
1999	34	21	6.5 million
2000	34	21	N/A

Note: Attendance figures are for the overall weekend
*Regular-season, or points races
Sources: NASCAR, Goodyear Auto Racing Attendance Report, and Street & Smith SPORTSBUSINESS JOURNAL research

NASCAR ON TV

How the Winston Cup Series television ratings have fared against major sports

BROADCAST NETWORKS

League	1993*	1994	1995	1996	1997	1998	1999	2000**
NFL	14.9	14.1	13.5	12.8	12.0	11.6	11.7	10.4
NASCAR	5.0	5.4	5.1	5.2	5.8	5.7	5.5	5.3
NBA	4.8	4.9	4.6	5.0	5.3	4.9	4.8	3.4
MLB	3.8	6.2	5.8	3.0	2.7	3.1	3.0	2.8
NHL	N/A	N/A	2.0	2.4	2.0	1.5	1.4	1.6

CABLE NETWORKS

League	1993*	1994	1995	1996	1997	1998	1999	2000**
NFL	7.9	9.8	8.6	7.7	7.5	8.1	8.2	8.6
NASCAR	3.1	3.2	3.9	4.0	4.3	4.0	4.1	4.0
NBA	1.7	1.8	1.8	1.7	2.0	1.7	1.7	1.3
MLB	1.7	1.9	1.7	1.6	1.5	1.9	1.5	1.3
NHL	N/A	1.1	0.9	0.6	0.8	0.7	0.6	0.6

N/A—Not available or not applicable
*The year indicates when a season ended; NBA ratings for 1996 are actually for the 1995-96 season, while NASCAR ratings are for the 1996 Winston Cup season.
**As of September 16, 2000.

NASCAR 'TOP FIVE'

Television ratings for NASCAR's five premier events

RACE	1994	1995	1996	1997	1998	1999	2000
Daytona 500	9.6	7.8	9.2	8.6	8.6	9.6	8.4
Coca-Cola 600	3.5	4.3	4.6	5.0	5.0	4.9	4.3
Brickyard 400	5.7	7.2	4.3	5.3	4.1	4.6	3.7
Pepsi Southern 400	3.2	3.4	3.8	4.5	3.9	4.6	2.6
Winston 500	3.7	5.2	5.5	4.1	4.3	4.0	3.9

Source: Nielsen Media Research
and Street & Smith SPORTSBUSINESS JOURNAL research

Right: Bill and Anne France pose before Bill's Mercury coupe after a race in 1939.

SPONSOR COSTS

Year	Primary Sponsor
1995	$5 million–$7 million
1996	$7 million–$9 million
1997	$8 million–$10 million
1998	$8 million–$10 million
1999	$10 million–$11 million
2000	$12 million
2001	$15 million

Source: Street & Smith
SPORTSBUSINESS JOURNAL research

RETAIL SALES

Year	Licensed sales
1995	$600 million
1996	$770 million
1997	$800 million
1998	$950 million
1999	$1.13 billion
2000	$1.2 billion*

*projected
Source: NASCAR

Another big number worth noting is the market capitalization of a publicly traded company whose fortunes are directly tied to NASCAR and vice versa. The nation's biggest track operator, International Speedway Corporation (Daytona, Talladega, Darlington, Michigan, Watkins Glen, and six others) has a market value (as of January 1, 2001) of over $2 billion—down almost 40 percent from its high, but still a big number. It should also be noted that NASCAR, which is the private property of the France family, owns 60 percent of International Speedway Corp.

Big numbers also include the rewards gained by Winston Cup competitors. Winston Cup's 2000 Series Champ Bobby Labonte won over $4 million in race purses last season, before picking up a check from R.J. Reynolds for over $3 million at the Winston Cup awards banquet in New York last December. Runner-up Dale Earnhardt had to settle for combined season and Winston winnings of $5,805,000. The twentieth-place finisher in the season championship, Jerry Nadeau, picked up over $2 million in prize money for his efforts.

Another place big numbers and NASCAR Winston Cup racing intersect is when sponsorship is discussed. Less than ten years ago, $3 million was the going rate to sponsor a front-running team. Now, the number is approaching $15 million, and there is no reason to believe that the cost of racing is going to go down.

Perhaps the biggest big number is defined by the symbiosis between NASCAR fans and companies involved in big time stock car racing. It is that phenomenon which explains the magnetic attraction that NASCAR has to major corporations that support NASCAR through car sponsorships, event sponsorships, TV and radio sponsorships, co-promotions, or licensed product agreements. The loyalty that NASCAR fans have toward companies that support their sport is irrefutably translated into money in the bank by companies, large and small.

In view of those big numbers, it is probably fair to ask how a regional activity, initially the provenance of bootleggers, rural mechanics, and daredevils became a mega-billion dollar colossus? How did NASCAR become a sport bigger than nearly any other in the land, motorized or otherwise?

There are a lot of explanations: fate, amazing foresight, a dedication to pleasing the fans based on close competition held in first-class facilities, and finally, three powerful forces of commerce that arrived at the same conclusion for the same reason. NASCAR is where the fans are. And the fans are where the money is. Which is why the automobile industry, television, and consumer brands converged to drive NASCAR to its current lofty status.

The road to this amazing success began in 1934, when Bill France, Sr., and his wife Anne (Bledsoe) left Washington, D.C., with 25 dollars and Bill's box of mechanic's tools in their car, eventually to arrive in Daytona Beach, Florida. Depending on which legend you choose to believe, the Frances settled here a.) because their car broke down and they didn't have the money to go on, or b.) because they fell in love with the beauty of the place and decided to stay.

Certainly Daytona's role in the world of motorsports would have been appealing to "Big Bill," a six-foot-five-inch mechanic who had raced in the Washington, D.C.,

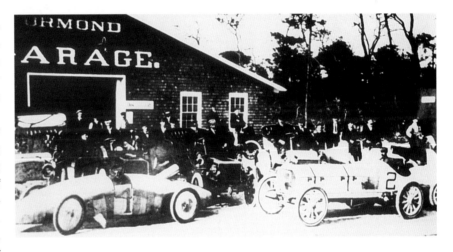

Left: John Rutherford pounds through the ruts on Daytona's Beach-Road course in 1936. Below: North of Daytona, Ormond Beach, Florida, was a haven for early gentlemen racers.

area before heading south. Daytona Beach in the mid-Thirties was the world's center of speed, the site for land-speed-record runs by the likes of Englishman Malcolm Campbell. By 1936, however, the quest for longer straightaways would lead speed merchants to places like the Bonneville Salt Flats for their record attempts.

To keep tourists coming, Daytona and Volusia county officials looked to promoters to run races that would bring big numbers of racing fans traveling to the "Beach." Using a 1.5-mile stretch of white sand and a parallel section of Highway A1A, the American Automobile Association sanctioned an event in 1936; Bill France finished fifth that day.

Even though Big Bill enjoyed some success as a racer, France had the foresight to see that the real opportunity for he and Anne was in promoting races, not driving in them. By 1938, the Frances were organizing races on the "Beach" and small tracks around the Southeast, bringing racing to a ready and willing audience. Purses frequently included treasures like a bottle of rum, a case of motor oil, a box of cigars, or an oil change at his gas station on Main Street.

Bill would do the organizing and promoting. Anne would do everything from ticket stubbing to the back-office work. Racers that ran with the Frances were sure to get paid—not always a certainty in early days of Southern racing. Soon, the Frances were earning the loyalty of the people who made the sport possible: the racers.

After the war, in 1946, Bill began promoting stock car races throughout the Southeast, quickly realizing that there was a need for a governing body that could bring some order to the loosely organized, some might say fly-by-night, racing tours that had sprung up in the region.

It was then that fate intervened in the person of the sports editor of the Charlotte, North Carolina, newspaper, Wilton Garrison. France met with him to try get interest in a story about an upcoming hundred-mile race he was promoting at the Charlotte Fairgrounds. As the story goes, Garrison told Big Bill that before he could expect to get papers interested in carrying stories about his races, he would need a well-defined racing series with consistent rules and a point structure that would fairly determine an overall national champion. Recognizing the wisdom of his comments, France returned to Daytona to establish the National Championship Stock Car Circuit for the 1947 season. His gas station was its headquarters, Anne was the chief operating officer, and they showed their flair for promotion with the slogan: "Where the fastest that run, run the fastest."

Before the year was out, France knew what to do next—form an association that would unite track opera-

France convened a meeting in December of 1947 that lasted four days and would forever shape the future of stock car racing in America.

Above: Pictured on the roof of the Streamline Hotel in Daytona Beach, the group that reorganized stock car racing in December 1947.

tors, drivers, car owners, and promoters to create a national sanctioning body to further his vision and rule the business of stock car racing.

To do this, France convened a meeting in December of 1947 that lasted for four days and would forever shape the future of stock car racing in America. The place was the Streamline Hotel on South Atlantic Avenue in Daytona Beach. The site was the top-floor Ebony Room. It has been reported that the gathering was a mixture of racers, mechanics, track owners, bootleggers, a turnip farmer, and assorted hustlers.

Regardless of the vocations of the attendees, the result of those meetings was the creation of the institution that defines the most popular form of automobile racing in America today. Here it was ordained that "present conditions would be improved" and that "after-race arguments" would be eliminated. Further, it was agreed that purses would be assured and drivers would get their winnings immediately after the race.

The organization to make this all possible would be called the National Association of Stock Car Auto Racing,

and its first commissioner would be E. G. "Cannonball" Baker. Membership cost was ten dollars, which brought with it a decal, a lapel pin, a membership card, and ten dollars' worth of coupons. In its first full year of operation, NASCAR sanctioned fifty-two races, nearly all of them in the Southeast.

Bill France not only understood the importance of published (and enforced) rules and regulations, he also understood that fans really wanted to see stock cars race, not the modifieds which made up the fields in NASCAR's early days. These coupes of '30s vintage with hopped-up motors were the children of necessity; the auto industry had not yet cranked up production after the conclusion of World War II, and current stock cars were scarce.

By 1949, NASCAR was ready to give the fans what they wanted, and the Frances took their show, headlined by "Strictly Stock" vehicles, to Charlotte for a 150-mile dirt track race. Fans started arriving at six in the morning, and by the time the race started, there were cars parked four miles away. An estimated 12,000 fans gave a rousing endorsement to Big Bill's stock car concept.

In the '50s, paved tracks began to appear, the first superspeedway was built (Darlington), and automobile manufacturers began to notice a correlation between a stock car's success on the track and its sales success on the showroom floor. The crowds grew, the series expanded, and NASCAR got a big boost in credibility as a national sanctioning body when Indianapolis-based AAA withdrew from the business of sanctioning races.

Before the decade was out, however, visible factory support diminished when, in 1957, the auto industry trade group AMA recommended that manufacturers reduce their roles in motorsports. But that didn't stop Bill France from building the track of his dreams, the Daytona International Speedway—a two-and-a-half-mile high-banked tri-oval the likes of which racing fans had never seen.

The '60s saw growth accelerate; more new tracks and more national exposure as NASCAR stock car racing now reached as far west as California and as far north as Maine. Ingenious car builders "interpreted" rules in ways NASCAR never imagined, and names like Fireball, Richard, Junior, and Cale started to appear in stories on sports pages all around the country. Soon television cameras started to focus on these daredevils' remarkable feats, occasionally broadcasting live segments or replaying events taped and edited to fit slots in anthology shows like ABC's Wide World of Sports.

None of this was lost on Detroit, as factory teams from Ford, Chevrolet, Pontiac, and Dodge returned to the fray with a vengeance, slugging it out for bragging rights every Sunday afternoon. National sponsors also took note, and suddenly the names of breweries, national financial institutions, and food companies began replacing the names of car dealers, service stations, and body shops on the flanks of the NASCAR fields.

By 1970, TV networks began to occasionally televise live flag-to-flag NASCAR action, their judgment reinforced by ever improving ratings. They didn't carry every race, but suddenly premier events like the Daytona 500 were sought after properties by all of the networks.

NASCAR's growing television exposure wasn't lost on the tobacco companies who had been legislated out of the medium. Big-time series sponsorship in the form of the R.J. Reynolds Company arrived to provide more than hefty purses and point funds. The Winston brand provided high-visibility promotion of the Winston Cup Series in national print media from the beginning of the season to the black-tie finale at New York's Waldorf-Astoria.

Now NASCAR was in the big leagues. Marketing giants like Proctor & Gamble and General Mills were taking notice and entering the sport as sponsors. Cable networks like ESPN, TNN, and TBS began carrying every Winston Cup race not carried by the big over-the-air networks like ABC and CBS.

Other NASCAR series, like the Busch Grand National and

Craftsman Truck Series, also started receiving live flag-to-flag coverage, as television's voracious appetite for original programming and new viewers fed on the excitement and accessibility of NASCAR racing.

The explosion in popularity seemed exponential, with more big time sponsors coming to the same conclusion; NASCAR means business. Big business. Retailers, cereal makers, fast food chains, phone companies, appliance makers, and more rushed to put their names and products in front of the fans.

The NASCAR Winston Cup season now stretches over eleven months, from preseason testing at Daytona in January to the black-tie gala celebrating the season's championship at the Waldorf in December. It is the longest season in all of professional sports.

Where will it all end? Like Bill France said in '48: "Stock car racing has boomed beyond anyone's wildest dreams, and I feel we are in for another big year." It's hard to disagree. ■

Left: Bill France, Sr. (left), Harry Hartz (center), and NASCAR's first commissioner, E.G. "Cannonball" Baker. Below: A Dodge pace car at Daytona. Bottom: NASCAR's first Strictly Stock race, Charlotte Speedway, 1949.

PHOTOS COURTESY OF NASCAR RACING ARCHIVES

SIR ISAAC NEWTON AND SANTA'S ELVES

Wind tunnel testing the Dodge Intrepid R/T. By William Neely

You might say the whole business of wind tunnel testing for the new Dodge Intrepid R/T race car boils down to two things: wiggle room and Sir Isaac Newton. You might also say that the guys at Auburn Hills, Michigan, are doing their homework. But what is the "homework," who are the "guys" and what is "wiggle room"? While we're at it, what does Sir Isaac Newton have to do with any of this?

Okay, fasten your seat belts. The "homework" is building an entire racing program from scratch. And not just any old racing program, one for NASCAR Winston Cup. Some companies might be satisfied with starting slowly and building up to a full head of steam, but not the Dodge boys; they're determined to get right out there and run with the big dogs from the beginning. None of this "stay under the front porch" thing for them.

The "guys" are a talented and highly interesting pack of engineers, dedicated to crafting one of the best race cars ever, right out of the box. Tim Culbertson, Dodge NASCAR Winston Cup program manager, who heads up the project, introduces the team: "When the race car program began a couple of years ago, Jeff Bordner was named senior aerodynamic development engineer, John Brzustowicz headed up the 3/8-scale model work, Todd Lounsberry was in charge of Computational Fluid Dynamics, Sandy Weinstein was assigned to full-scale wind-tunnel testing and parts manufacturing, and Terry Dekoninck worked on driver cooling.

"We built a 'one team' concept for all of our individual teams with Sandy [Weinstein] as the lead dog on the aerodynamics program," says Culbertson. "The major contacts with the actual race teams are Kurt Romberg at Petty Enterprises, Todd Holbert at Bill Davis Racing, and Bill Deese at Ray Evernham Motorsports."

The term "wiggle room" is one Culbertson uses to describe the infinitesimal latitude NASCAR rules allow for manufacturers and race teams to work their personal black magic on aerodynamics, that tiny tolerance allowed in the templates with which they can try to squeeze out, say, a thousandth of a second.

John Brzustowicz works with the 3/8-scale model of the Intrepid in the wind tunnel. On the laptop computer to his right is a tool called Wake Imaging, which allows testers to visualize the air pressure around the model.

Above: Dodge's Todd Lounsberry (standing) and Jean-Michel Esclafer de la Rode. Below and bottom right: In September 2000, NASCAR mandated the use of a two-inch-high strip on the roof of Winston Cup cars, sending the Dodge team back to the wind tunnel for more testing.

Templates are the rigid aluminum gauges that conform to the exact shape of the race car's body. They are formed from a showroom car and guarded closely by tech officials. But it hasn't always been this way. In 1962 when Smokey Yunick, the master magician of mechanics, had trouble in tech inspection at Daytona, he was told to take his car back to his garage on the other side of Daytona Beach and "make it right." After several hours of laboring by Smokey and his crew, he went back and asked if could borrow the templates, "just to make sure."

His crew began to build the car to fit the templates, but as Smokey assessed the situation he said, "Wait a minute, boys. We're going about this all wrong. What we need to do is change the templates." So they modified the templates to fit Smokey's black and gold Pontiac.

It was the last time NASCAR ever let the templates out of its sight. Today's tech crew is far more strict.

"NASCAR has the toughest restrictions [in aerodynamics] in all of racing, but there still is room for engineering and creativity," says Culbertson.

"From the beginning, our program has been full-scale wind tunnel testing, 3/8-scale tunnel testing, and computational fluid dynamics, which, simply stated, means wind tunnel in a computer," he explains. "We combine all of this with track testing and then we work with the teams.

"There are two kinds of engineers, in my opinion: One is the J. C. Whitney type, the one whose knowledge is based upon experience. If something occurs he goes into his head and pulls down what he thinks is a good solution, something that has solved the problem in the past. Then there is the the engineer by degree, the F equals M times A type [Newton's second law of motion: force equals mass times acceleration].

"The race teams bring a lot of the experience-type engineers—who know what worked and what didn't—in contact with the engineers by degree, who might be better trained in the principals of engineering. Putting these two together is what we think is a classic example of two plus two being equal to five. We're all bringing something to the party."

When working with such small numbers as hundredths and thousandths of a mile per hour, Culbertson feels the DaimlerChrysler Technical Center's 3/8-scale wind tunnel may be the most helpful. "The major benefit is that we can do things a lot quicker," he says. "It's the most important thing we brought from our passenger-car program. The detail is outstanding on the model cars [roughly the size of a go-kart] from the underbody to the engine compartment. It's hard to imagine how fine the models are. I used to be manager of the department that built these components, and every time I walked in I had a feeling I was watching Santa's elves making toys. Everything is perfect but miniature. The knowledge of the fidelity required to have good models has always been important to us."

The engineers have learned a lot from the full-scale wind tunnel, which belongs to Lockheed (DaimlerChrysler's own $50 million, full-scale wind tunnel will be up and running next year), but Culbertson says they've learned more by listening than leading.

The ability and the desire to learn things, even if they are out of the realm which is considered the norm, has led the team to many startling discoveries about aerodynamics and the race car.

Above: Ganassi Racing's Andy Graves. Facing page: Precise measurements of Ganassi's Coors Light–sponsored car are taken in order to make sure it conforms to NASCAR's templates.

"We listen to our teams, people like Kurt Romberg at Petty, who is an aerodynamicist by profession, about what they are doing with radiators and things like that. Then we start to develop our own opinion. Actually, we listen to what the racing world is doing, and then we try to figure what we can do to make a difference."

But what exactly are the engineers looking for in wind tunnel testing? "The major things are drag force numbers and, more important, the balance of down force numbers, front and rear, that will directly affect how the vehicle handles, tight and loose.

"We design two more-or-less-distinct race cars: the superspeedway car and the short-track car. On superspeedways all you have to worry about is drag," Culbertson points out. "At Talladega, for example, they never lift [the accelerator]; they give up down force for low drag. On short tracks, you want as much down force as possible. On intermediate tracks it's obviously a combination of the two, but it becomes a real art to determine what they want and what they need for each particular track. That's where the wind tunnel is extraordinary.

"We also do tunnel tests of the car at different yaw angles, making sure it has the right numbers, not only straight ahead, but in the turns."

Wind-tunnel testing is a complex business: In addition to down force, drag, and yaw, the aero engineers have to make sure spin aerodynamics is right so that the roof flaps work to keep the car from flipping in a spin. They run tests for qualifying as well as for race day, and they test for cooling capabilities and for the flow of fluids, both from the radiator into the engine and from the intake manifold into the cylinders. They even test for driver cooling.

The Dodge Winston Cup team also uses the wind tunnel for Wake Imaging, which is a system co-developed with Boeing, where they can actually see a color picture on the computer and can determine by the computerized color of the air at certain points if it is high or low pressure. They might find that the air is going someplace they don't want it to go so they can make the necessary changes to body shape to redirect the flow.

"When everything we do is brought into the equation, it becomes two plus two plus two equals eight," Culbertson says. "Sometimes it's what we call the 'eureka!' syndrome. I mean, we work away and work away and all of a sudden its 'Whoa, look at this!'"

It is perhaps this eureka syndrome that has propelled the Dodge boys toward their dream of their first checkered flag in Winston Cup. It all begins when the green flag drops for the Daytona 500 on February 18, 2001.

The ability and the desire to learn things, even if they are out of the realm which is considered the norm, has led the team to many startling discoveries about aerodynamics and the race car. Tens of thousands of man hours, computer time, and wind-tunnel testing have gone into their new racing program.

"We're very confident that with the smarts from my team and the smarts from their team [the Dodge race teams], we can compete with anybody," Culbertson says, with the pride of a father whose son has just blasted a home run in his first game with the New York Yankees.

Santa's elves are standing by the wind tunnel right now, and they will be ready to go. They will not be neophytes when the first green flag drops. ∎

DODGE NASCAR V-8

Dodge gets ready to make some noise. By Kevin Clemens

Every racing car is defined by its engine. The screaming V-12 of a Ferrari, the booming V-10 of a Viper, or the high pitched whine of an Indy-car engine are all part of the visceral appeal that thrills crowds and warms hearts. NASCAR has its own special sound—a resonance that shakes your insides and assaults your body. Watch the crowd as forty distinctly American engines are fired up on a Sunday afternoon. As one the crowd rises to its feet in awe as the waves of sound wash over them. This is what they have come for. For years, that cacophony has come from Chevrolet and Ford and Pontiac. Very soon, the rumbling noise will also come from an all-new NASCAR racing engine from Dodge.

It won't be the first time that Chrysler has competed in America's own motorsport. In the early days of stock-car racing in the Fifties, the 331-cubic-inch Hemi engine was all conquering. Drivers like Lee Petty pushed the big Mopars to victory after victory. Again in the mid-Sixties, the racing Hemi was the engine to beat and helped to crown Richard Petty "the King." By the mid-Seventies, however, the company seemed to lose interest in racing in general, and the NASCAR program quietly died. Few thought they would ever see a Dodge back on the high banks of Talladega or Darlington.

Ted Flack was part of the Chrysler NASCAR program in the 1970s. He started out as a mechanic running the engine dynamometers and ended up as a test engineer, helping to create the special parts that are needed to keep a racing program flourishing. At the end of Chrysler's NASCAR involvement in 1979, he moved to designing prototype engines, including the aluminum block engines that power most of Chrysler's fleet. Today, Ted Flack has a dream job as Dodge's manager of NASCAR engine programs.

The Dodge NASCAR engine program officially started on October 14, 1999. Until that time, Dodge had been successfully involved with the NASCAR Craftsman Truck Series, but its connection to Winston Cup racing was only a distant memory. On the surface, NASCAR's rules for manu-

facturer participation seem pretty straightforward. The engine must be based on a production engine with respect to bore centers, camshaft location, deck height of the block, and height of the intake manifold. The engine block must be cast iron, the heads can be aluminum, and the engine can displace no more than 358 cubic inches. Engines must run with a specified carburetor, and fuel injection is strictly prohibited. Also prohibited is the use of hemispherical combustion chambers, so Dodge will be returning to the superspeedways without its favorite Hemi. Instead, the Dodge NASCAR engine is based on the 5.7-liter Dodge truck engine. This deep-skirt block design has robust six-bolt main bearings and makes a good start for a NASCAR racing engine. A manufacturer such as Dodge is responsible for supplying NASCAR-approved engine blocks, cylinder heads, and intake manifolds. Each team's engine builder chooses whatever crankshaft, pistons, valvetrain, and camshaft he feels will win races.

In spite of the apparent simplicity of the project, the fierce competitiveness of

Left to right: Dave Eovaldi (standing), Patrick Baer, and David James are members of DaimlerChrysler's Powertrain Engineering team, assigned to develop Dodge's NASCAR engine.

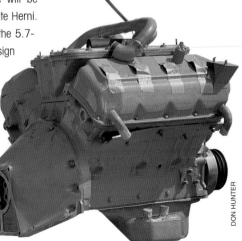

DON HUNTER

The NASCAR block was designed from the start for use with a dry sump system, rather than adapting a block designed for a traditional engine with an oil pan.

NASCAR racing has demanded the application of some of DaimlerChrysler's highest technologies. "It's extremely high tech because you have to optimize all of the parts within the rules," admits Flack. "Refinement is the word," he adds. Flack has had the assistance of almost every department within DaimlerChrysler's formidable Technical Center in Auburn Hills, Michigan. All parts for the engine have been designed with the help of the corporation's powerful computers. Finite element analysis allows the internal stresses to be analyzed before parts are built, and rapid prototyping allows engineers to have prototype parts built and in their hands literally overnight. "If there is a lab here, we are using it," says Flack about the Daimler-Chrysler Tech Center.

If all of the corporate involvement seems overkill, consider how NASCAR racing engines have changed since the mid-Seventies. At that time a strong engine would produce around 550 to 600 horsepower at 6000 rpm. Today, a NASCAR engine produces more than 780 horsepower from the same displacement pushrod engine at 9000 rpm. Last year, good engines produced about 750 horsepower, and next year everyone is expecting another 10 to 20 horsepower increase.

The design for the components that Dodge will supply has been thoroughly investigated, and many special features have been incorporated. Most teams running Chevrolet and Ford engines, for example, run piston squirters that send a jet of oil against the bottom of the piston to aid in cooling and improve longevity. Usually this entails plumbing special oil lines inside the engine to bring the high-pressure oil to the places it's needed. Dodge's engine designers built oil passages into the NASCAR engine block to provide outlets for the squirters while doing away with the added plumbing. The NASCAR block was

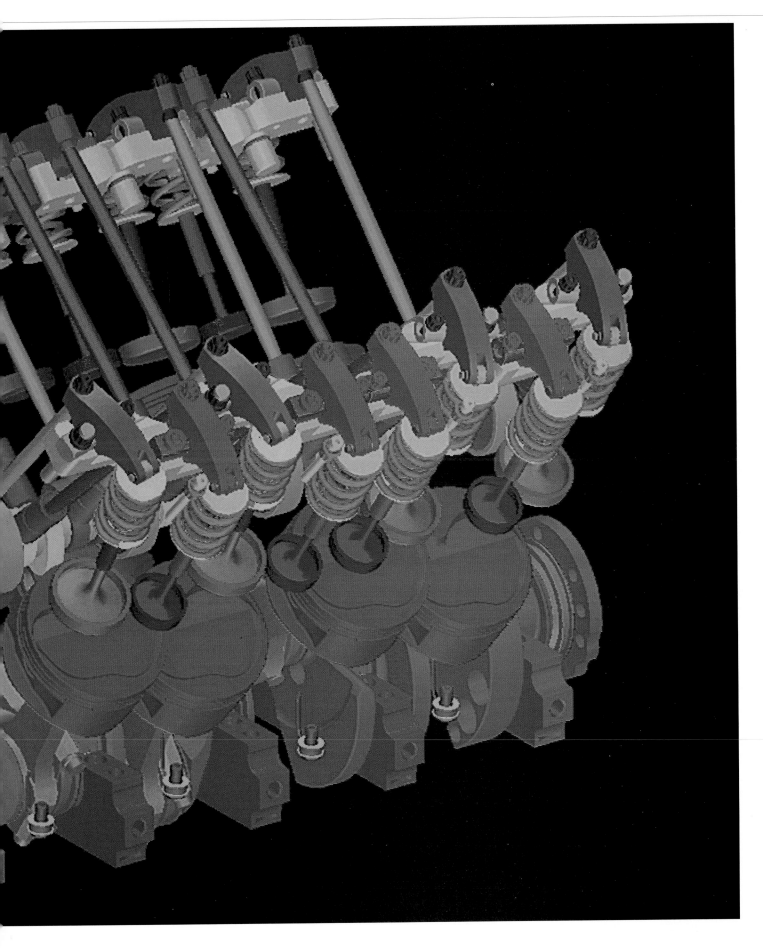

Chrysler Hemi

By Kevin Clemens

Chrysler's factory involvement in performance has its roots in the early 1950s, when the Chrysler Firepower V-8 was introduced. This 331-cubic-inch engine was the automaker's first V-type engine and featured hemispherical combustion chambers in its cylinder heads. The "Hemi" design provided superior combustion through better breathing and a more optimal central location of the spark plug when compared with the other performance engines that Detroit was producing. The Hemi took five years to develop and in its 1951 guise made 180 horsepower, making it the most powerful passenger-car engine produced by an American manufacturer. The Hemi quickly began its domination of NASCAR racing, and the engine stayed around until 1958, with the 392-cubic-inch street version producing 390 horsepower with a pair of four-barrel carburetors.

In 1957, however, the Automobile Manufacturing Association (AMA) passed a ban on factory involvement in racing by its members. There was fear of a public outcry and government involvement in safety, and the growing horsepower race among the Big Three was an easy target. But automakers knew that performance would sell cars and continued to provide under-the-table parts and help to the racing community. Finally, Ford publicly defied the ban with its 352-cubic-inch "Special Power" engine. Chevrolet and Pontiac followed quickly with their 409-cubic-inch engines, and the race was on once again.

Chrysler only had a 383-cubic-inch engine with a conventional wedge cylinder head to compete. Development of that design led to the 413- and 426-cubic-inch Max Wedge engines of the early Sixties. These engines met with significant success in both NASCAR and drag racing, dominating the Super Stock class. But Chrysler still had the Hemi ace up its sleeve.

On February 23, 1964, Chrysler reintroduced the Hemi at the Daytona 500. It was an auspicious debut, with 426-cubic-inch Hemi-powered cars finishing first, second, third, and fourth. With the block and bottom end based upon the successful 426-cubic-inch Max Wedge engine, the new Hemi was an outright racing engine with aluminum cylinder heads, radical cam timing, an unheated aluminum intake manifold, and high 12.5:1 compression ratio. In the face of a phenomenally successful season, NASCAR called foul, insisting that Chrysler would have to produce several thousand engines for sale in a production vehicle in order to be legal for stock car racing. Chryslers were banned for the 1965 season, and racing suffered. To be allowed back in, the company bravely began production of a detuned street version of the 426 Hemi with lower compression cast-iron cylinder heads, different valve timing, hydraulic valve lifters, and more civilized intake and exhaust manifolds. These engines found their way into a variety of Dodge and Plymouth models, becoming the mainstay of Chrysler's muscle car program.

But it was the racing version of the 426-cubic-inch Hemi that was setting records and making headlines. Rated by the company at 425 horsepower at 5000 rpm and 490 pound-feet of torque at 4000 rpm, those figures were highly suspect. The government and insurance companies were keeping a close watch on the auto industry and the resumption of the horsepower race. The street versions probably produced closer to 500 horsepower, and the NASCAR racing version of the 426-cubic-inch engine must have been pushing more than 750 horsepower. Just as in the original Hemi from the Fifties, the Sixties variety used a pair of rocker shafts to actuate the valves and placed the spark plug in the middle of the combustion chamber for efficient ignition. The hemispherical shaped combustion chambers benefited from a serious scientific study of airflow, courtesy of Chrysler's science laboratory. This wasn't a program run by a bunch of grease monkeys.

The Hemi's reign in NASCAR was ended in the 1970s by a rule change, and the street production Hemi followed it in 1971, killed by high manufacturing costs and a new emphasis on fuel economy and exhaust emissions. But the Hemi lives on today in the aftermarket; aluminum-block versions of the engine power Top Fuel dragsters and Funny Cars and everything else from drag-boats to monster trucks. Chrysler itself began remanufacturing Hemi components in 1993; today, armed with a Mopar Performance parts catalog and a good machine shop, a new Hemi can be brought to life for about $10,000.

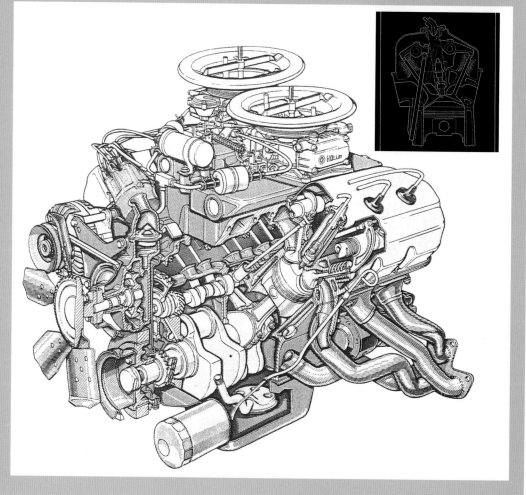

also designed from the start for use with a dry sump system, rather than adapting a block designed for a traditional engine with an oil pan.

The cooling system has also received enormous scrutiny. A water manifold that supplies precisely calculated amounts of water throughout the block results in a temperature difference of less than three degrees anywhere in the engine block.

The idea is to build components that will allow high horsepower capability and will last all of a 500- or even 600-mile race in the heat of summer. The life expectancy of an engine block is 3000 racing miles. Engines will be rebuilt after every race with new pistons, valves, and rocker arms. Components like crankshafts also last 3000 miles, while connecting rods have a racing life of 1500 miles.

The real key to power production will be the cylinder heads and valvetrain. Because NASCAR requires restrictor plates at superspeedways like Daytona, different heads and intake manifolds are used at these tracks. That means completely different flow speeds of air through the engine must be accommodated, and the valve geometry is con-

siderably different than at tracks where engines run unrestricted. The NASCAR regulations on camshaft design make it difficult to keep everything together at the 9300 rpm that the engines can see during a race. "Keeping the valve springs in the engine and the valve heads attached to the valves is pretty important, but hard to do," admits Dodge's NASCAR engine program manager. Flack has one man in his five-person team who works just on valvetrain design with all of the teams.

The first engines for the new Dodge NASCAR program were built last May. Since that time, five racing teams have been busy building and testing the engines that they will be racing with this season. As they have in other kinds of racing, most notably Vipers in sports car racing, Dodge Motorsports has instituted a "one-team" approach. Each of the five racing teams has been sharing what it discovers in building and testing the engines with each of the other teams. It is a remarkable show of trust and cooperation in a business that is renowned for its competitive nature. The result has been more than 150 people around the country working on the task of building a NASCAR racing engine that will be competitive right out of the box. It

Neil Van Arsdol (above) is a model fabricator whose work in rapid prototyping of experimental parts has sped the development of the NASCAR engine.

Chrysler Max Wedge
By Kevin Clemens

Between the successful racing Chrysler Hemi of the 1950s and the even more successful racing Chrysler Hemi of the 1960s, there was an engine that kept the Dodge and Chrysler name afloat in the performance market. After the AMA ban on manufacturer involvement in racing in 1957, Chrysler lost interest in the original Hemi engine that had served it so well since 1951. By 1959 the Hemi was dead, and when Ford, Chevrolet, and Pontiac began to defy the racing ban in 1960, Chrysler only had its 383-cubic-inch V-8 engine to work with. It didn't seem like much, but the crafty engineers at Chrysler had some ideas that would eventually make the engine into a power giant.

The engineers started with a wild Ram Induction setup that placed two Carter four-barrel carburetors on 30-inch-long crossed intake manifolds. The intake runners were so long that the carbs actually sat suspended over the front inner fenders. Low-end torque was this intake system's long suit, and the Ram Induction 383 won nine NASCAR races in its first year. But that was just the beginning.

For 1962, Chrysler designed a proper racing engine, called the Max Wedge because of its wedge-shaped combustion chamber. Displacing 413 cubic inches, this was an engine designed for both drag racing and stock car racing. Inside the engine were beefed-up oiling and valve gear components, upgraded intake and exhaust valves, a baffled oil pan, and a stainless steel head gasket. Pistons were forged and available in 11.0:1 and 13.5:1 compression ratios. The crossed aluminum intake manifolds were again used, but this time they measured a shorter fifteen inches in length with a Carter four-barrel carburetor mounted on a plenum at each end of the manifold. Maybe the most distinctive part of the engine was a pair of huge cast-iron exhaust manifolds that swept upward over the fender wells to carry exhaust gases into three-inch head pipes. The

413-cubic-inch Max Wedge engine was rated at 410 horsepower at 5400 rpm with the 11.0:1 compression ratio and 420 horsepower at 5400 rpm when the 13.5:1 compression pistons were used. The numbers were very conservative. In 1962, four class records were set in NHRA drag racing by the 413-cubic-inch Max Wedge.

In 1963, the Max Wedge grew to 426 cubic inches, thanks to an increase in cylinder bore from 4.19 inches to 4.25 inches. These engines were called Stage II, and things were getting serious. For drag racing, a pair of Carter four-barrel carburetors were used, while the NASCAR engines used a single four-barrel carb. With this engine, and helped out by the use of lightweight aluminum front ends, trunk mounted batteries, and other lightweight parts, Chrysler products completely dominated the Super Stock classes in NHRA drag racing. Additional top-end power made the company competitive with Ford and Chevrolet in NASCAR. The

twin-carburetor setup was rated at 425 horsepower at 5600 rpm, a figure that was clearly under-reporting the engine's capabilities.

The final Max Wedge engine, the Stage III, was introduced in 1964, in the shadow of the reintroduction of the Chrysler Hemi. The Stage III engine featured a revised cylinder head and a different camshaft design. Although the Wedge had been incredibly successful in drag racing, it didn't do as well in NASCAR. Chrysler's answer was to bring back a hemispherical combustion chamber and place it atop the Max Wedge bottom end.

Ultimately, the Hemi would seal the fate of the Max Wedge. But it was the Wedge engine that gave Chrysler its performance start in the 1960s and helped engineers develop the camshaft designs, valvetrains and port shapes, and bottom-end reliability that allowed the Hemi engine to become dominant in stock car and drag racing until the end of the 1960s.

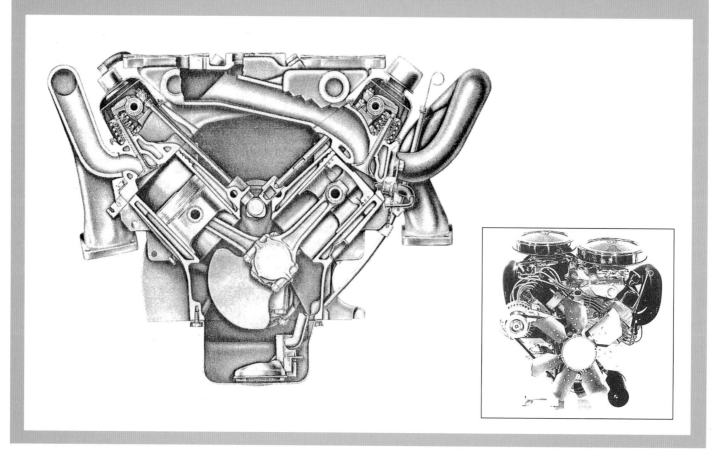

has also resulted in some strange combinations when the cylinder head from one shop is bolted to the engine block built by another team and is tested on the dynamometer of a third team. Flack says getting all of the teams to trust one another and work together might be the biggest accomplishment of all.

Terry Elledge has fifteen seasons of NASCAR racing experience and is the head of the engine program at Bill Davis Racing for drivers Ward Burton and Dave Blaney. He agrees that there has been cooperation between the Dodge teams but knows there will be a limit to this information exchange. "Initially what happens is everyone gets together and decides what should be done," said Elledge. "In the development process there is a lot of sharing, but it's a performance industry and at some point competition takes over," he adds. Elledge is particularly impressed by the access to technology he has had from the Dodge engineers. "We ask them something, they go back to their labs, do a study, and get back to us a week later with an answer," said Elledge.

Working with NASCAR has also been a pleasant experience for the Dodge engine team. In order to be acceptable for racing, the design of all Dodge supplied components must be submitted to and approved by NASCAR. The racing organization has in the past had a reputation for being somewhat difficult to work with, but Flack and his team have found the process to be quite straightforward. "We have been in close contact with them, showing them what we are planning to do and sharing the results with them," says Flack.

With all of this high-level development going on, it might be surprising to learn that the engine components are for sale over the counter. This is in fact a NASCAR rule, requiring parts to be readily available. Engine blocks cost about $4000, cylinder heads are about $1000 each, and intake manifolds are between $500 and $600. A racing team will use about twenty-five engines per year, and with five teams and all of the testing, the production of engines comes close to what DaimlerChrysler might build in the development of a prototype production engine. The company has hired a small foundry to produce the parts it needs for the NASCAR program. Eventually, development will include involvement in the lesser NASCAR series including trucks. There is also a possibility that an aluminum block version of the engine could be produced for sports car racing.

Since the first engines began running last May, testing has been almost nonstop. DaimlerChrysler's programmable dynamometers can be used to simulate an entire race with pit stops and yellow flags. But the real testing needs to take place on the racetrack, and more than 3000 miles in 500-mile tests have been accomplished. Most of the track testing has taken place at Kentucky's 1.5-mile oval speedway, which offers a good combination of speed, acceleration, and cornering. The development program was grueling, especially for teams that were also committed to the full 2000 NASCAR season.

For an engineer, racing is both very simple and very difficult. The goal is clear: You need to win. The schedule is straightforward: The race is held on Sunday, and it won't wait for you to find the best solution if it takes you until the following Tuesday. The difficult part comes when you realize that several dozen other race engineers around the country are trying to do the same thing, only just a bit better. The pressure is enormous. But the rewards of an all-new program are significant, too. "This is a new challenge for us, an opportunity to try new things," says Elledge. "We are just going to have to go down a development trail and see where it leads us." The only certainty is that success will require long hours and hard work. The engineers at Dodge Motorsports and the NASCAR Winston Cup teams have put both into the creation of their new engine. Now it remains to be seen if they have built a winner. ∎

Based on the 5.7-liter Dodge truck engine, the NASCAR engine will produce in excess of 750 horsepower. Per NASCAR regulations, all engine components are for sale over the counter.

THE 200-MPH ATHLETES

There's a lot more to driving a stock car than just stomping the gas pedal and turning left. By Michael Jordan

The in-car camera sweeps across the cockpit—and there's the driver, an otherworldly figure trapped in an unfriendly web of steel tubes, hydraulic lines, and electrical whatnot. There's nothing much going on, unless you happen to notice that the horizon has been flipped over to an impossible angle while the scenery zips past as if it were playing in the fast-forward mode. And yet the driver seems to just hang there in his seatbelts, apparently no more involved with what's going on than a kid playing a video game.

But when Jacques Dallaire, a specialist in sports performance, looks into the cockpit of a NASCAR racer, he sees something entirely different. "Drivers are athletes," he says. "There's no question about it."

Dallaire is in a position to know. Over the past decade, he and his colleagues at Human Performance International in Huntersville, North Carolina, have evaluated nearly 500 drivers from different forms of motorsport and compared their performances to those of athletes in conventional sports. "In NASCAR Winston Cup racing," Dallaire notes, "some events can last up to three hours. Our research over the years indicates that the heart rate response of drivers in high-performance motor racing like this reaches a level equal to approximately 82 percent of the driver's individual maximum heart-rate capacity, which is about 163 beats per minute. At 200 mph, the car travels the length of a football field every second, so the driver has to make decisions in thousandths of a second. In the corners, the g-loads might be three times the force of gravity, so a driver's head, which normally weighs about fifteen pounds, plus a five-pound helmet, might weigh sixty pounds under this influence. And the driver has to withstand these forces for hundreds of laps. Once you put all these things together, there's no question but that drivers are real athletes."

As with any racing car, the cockpit of a stock car is an incredibly noisy place, and the vibration is unrelenting. It's one thing to turn the wheel and stomp the pedals while at the wheel of an arcade game, but it's quite another, Dallaire points out, to perform in the harsh environment of a Winston Cup car, especially with forty other cars on the track at the same time.

First of all, there's the heat. Ambient temperatures can be exceptionally high during the long, hot summer of the Winston Cup season. Then there's the additional heat produced by an engine. All that heat in the front of the car is forced back toward the cockpit by the airstream, and the firewall gets so hot that drivers have to wear special heat-resistant cups over the heels of their racing shoes. Moreover, there's the heat from the exhaust system, plus the heat from engine oil and transmission oil, which is often routed through coolers within the cockpit. Even worse, the roof of a typical stock car tends to trap all of this heat within the cockpit, because the sleek aerodynamic shapes of modern Winston Cup cars permit far less air circulation into the cockpit than you'd expect, even at 200 mph. And finally, the driver's own body produces an enormous amount of heat because the heart has to pump so hard and fast to maintain blood circulation under the stress of the g-forces produced by the car.

When it comes to the physical test that stock car driving represents, Dallaire also notes that the presence of carbon monoxide is one particularly insidious aspect of the oval-track racing environment. "On a still day, a high-banked short track can become a soup bowl of exhaust gases," he says. "It's not too bad for the people in the pits, but for the drivers, who are racing literally nose-to-tail, it's like sucking on a car's tailpipe for an afternoon."

Aside from the feats of physical endurance that stock car driving requires, there are psychological challenges as well. Over the past thirty years, many psychological studies of racing drivers have been conducted, and a number of generalizations can be made. For example, racing drivers are mentally very quick, which correlates with high intelligence. Drivers have equally quick reaction times, under a quarter of a second, which is about as fast as the human nervous system can react. Drivers also have an

Physical endurance, quick reaction times, and an ability to withstand extreme stress are just some of the attributes that a racing driver needs in order to compete successfully in the harsh cockpit environment of a Winston Cup racing car.

excellent sense of what their bodies are doing, they are able to withstand extreme stress, and are extremely confident. Human Performance International's research, Dallaire says, has also revealed that the ability to concentrate is one of the defining characteristics of a top-rated racing driver.

"No other area of sport competition places the same demands on concentration that motor racing does," says Dallaire. "A driver must also maintain a high intensity of concentration for a long period of time without the benefit of half-time breaks, shift changes, or time-outs. In addition, the consequences of inattention can be disastrous." HPI also distinguishes between focused attention and generalized attention. A racer uses focused attention to improve some aspect of his driving, while generalized attention comes into play while tracking traffic, responding to radio calls from the pit crew, and planning strategy. "Racing drivers really have a remarkable ability to shift their concentration from one thing to another," Dallaire says. Indeed Dallaire and his colleagues at HPI have come to believe so strongly in the impact of concentration on overall performance that they have developed MindSHAPER, a computer software program that not only measures concentration skills but also improves them—something useful for anyone, not just race drivers.

Ironically, the drivers themselves have been among the last to acknowledge the athletic demands of their sport.

You can understand why when you remember that the NASCAR Winston Cup season has become virtually a year-round enterprise. Time is the one thing that no Winston Cup driver has enough of, and this makes it difficult to maintain the serious physical and mental conditioning that is necessary to perform at a peak level. Things are changing, however. A growing number of teams have already undertaken physical training for both drivers and pit crews, and psychological and performance training like that offered by HPI is a growing trend.

You don't have to look very hard to find evidence of NASCAR's profound influence on racing in this country. You can measure it by the money involved in NASCAR's new television broadcast contract. You can measure it by the number of paved oval tracks built over the last five years, the most intense period of speedway construction in this country since the great board tracks were erected in the Teens and Twenties. You can even measure it in terms of jobs and money. *Performance Racing Industry,* a magazine devoted to the commercial aspect of racing, estimates that some 403,000 people in the United States derive their incomes exclusively from racing, and these people help make the sport a $4.3 billion industry in this country. But most of all, you can measure NASCAR's importance by the caliber of driver it attracts. Its 200-mph athletes are clearly something special. ∎

DIGITAL DESIGN
AND THE TRON-FLAVORED WATER COOLER
By Reilly P. Brennan

Could the mouse be mightier than the monkey wrench? At the vast Daimler-Chrysler Tech Center in Auburn Hills, Michigan, it would seem that the business of building NASCAR Winston Cup race cars is increasingly more tron than it is turning ratchets. With more than 50 percent of the development of the Intrepid R/T Cup car accomplished on a computer screen, few steps in the engineering process remain that can't be tuned, tweaked, or tested by the click of a mouse.

But for Tim Culbertson, program manager for Dodge's Winston Cup racing program, the thronged technology doesn't belie the human experience, it actually requires of development an even more soulful interaction and involvement. "The computer has taken away a lot of the physical demands of design," he says. "But it's made it even more mental."

Culbertson and his team of twelve engineers (not including managers) haven't had time to take their heads out of the game. Starting with less than 500 days to get a brand-new race car and engine ready for one of the most competitive series in the world, they called upon the latest and greatest from the gee-whiz world of computer-aided technologies to help beat their deadline. Surprisingly, these applications all come from and are used in production car development, just tweaked-up slightly for a car that will travel at 200 mph at three times the force of gravity.

"If we didn't have these technologies it would easily take four to six times as long to produce a race car at the quality we're running," he says. "There's a real push of speed to market, and it's all these tools that allow us to get it done."

It's no surprise that some of the hottest technology in NASCAR would geyser from the Tech Center at Daimler-Chrysler's Auburn Hills headquarters. Originally completed in 1991 to the tune of $140 million, today's Tech Center is even bigger than the original 500,000-square-foot structure. Since its completion, an additional $370 million have been spent on improvements.

"There are three legs to the stool of what we're doing here: engine, aerodynamics, and chassis," Culbertson says. "We couldn't do it all without the Tech Center." With five laboratories, Dodge engineers have enlisted the help of the Aerodynamic and Computational Fluid Dynamics Lab, the Environmental Test Center, the Electromagnetic Compatibility Center, the Noise, Vibration and Harshness Lab, and the Powertrain Test Facility.

Zippy acronyms like DMA, FDM, LOM, and CFD fly around in conversation with Culbertson, a veritable translator of Dodge-speak for the uninitiated. It's probably easier for these to be communicated in short—all their real names unfold like disassembled origami into longer, polysyllabic names of gadgets, thingamajigs, and processes. And with the Daytona 500 approaching like the rising sun, there's little time to waste on semantics.

One of the most important tools for the development of the NASCAR Intrepid R/T is the Digital Modeling Assembly (DMA). It's just a basic design tool, but it makes amazingly clear sense of CATIA CAD/CAM/CAE—the ubiquitous software that permeates through nearly all strata of engineering on a computer at Dodge's formidable Technical Center. While CAD's usefulness is felt throughout the entire engineering process, it turns out to be a bit clunky when plopped on a computer screen, showing nothing more than lines that make vague shapes and curves. "DMA fills in the lines of CAD," Culbertson says. "It's an incredible visualizer for us."

More important, DMA allows Dodge engineers to view the entire race car, pick it apart on a computer screen, turn it around, and zoom inside to check part clearance even before a single piece is put together on a real-life model.

While the DMA allows on-screen analysis of the working insides of the NASCAR Intrepid R/T, CFD—Computational Fluid Dynamics—gives engineers information on the car's response to its surroundings. "I'd call CFD the wind tunnel on the computer," Culbertson says. The engine-performance software gives amazingly accurate (within ten percent of real-world numbers) data on the flow of air and fuel through the intake manifold and the flow of oil through the block and head.

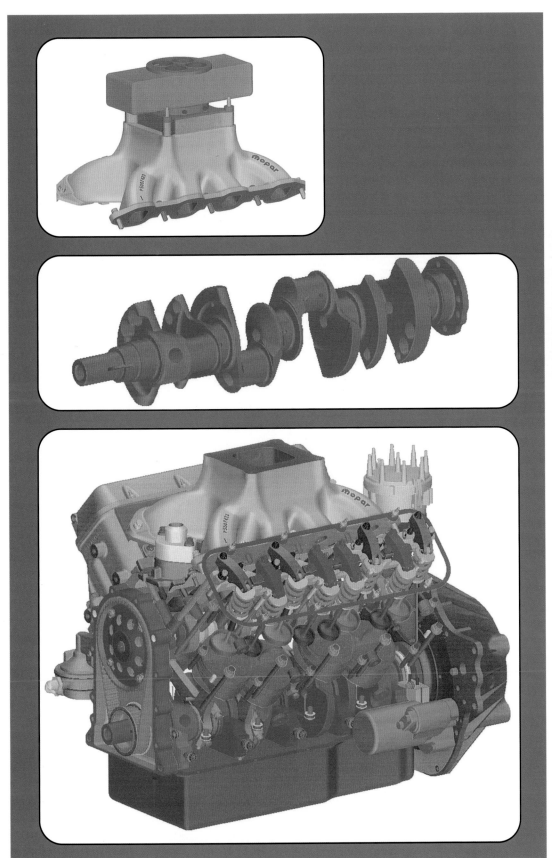

Above: David James,
a member of Dodge's
Powertrain Engineering team.
Top, left, and below: A tool
called Digital Modeling
Assembly, or DMA, allows
James's team to quickly
design and prototype
the various parts of the
engine on the Dodge
Intrepid R/T Cup car.

But ten percent can mean the difference between leader and loser in a series as competitive as NASCAR. So Dodge engineers eventually take their data to an actual 3/8-scale model of the Winston Cup Intrepid R/T. These smaller testings are typically run with wind simulating 130 mph, although true-to-track NASCAR speeds of close to 180 mph can be produced with accuracy. With changes made at a low-cost scale on the 3/8-scale model, Dodge has managed to save time and money on the actual tear-assing, true-to-life Winston Cup Intrepid R/T.

The path of the engineering process for the Winston Cup Intrepid R/T seems to snowball as time passes—computer technologies amass until the small models are tested; eventually a life-sized model of the car and its parts are produced using burnt paper. Yes, paper.

The Laminated Object Manufacturing (LOM) process is a key step in the rapid prototyping of the race car. By building a model by cutting and fusing layers of paper, a fin-

ished model of parts eventually appears. Due to the laser beam that cuts the paper, its edges are brown and the final product resembles a wood carving.

Possibly for the first time in Dodge's engineering history, these Space Age technologies mesh naturally with the youth of Culbertson's engineering team, the average age of which hovers somewhere in the range of late-twenties to early-thirties. "Engineers now really have computers almost from the womb," he says. "Most of these guys probably had Fisher-Price toys that were computerized. The computer to a twenty-two-year-old engineer is almost equal to an arm or a leg." Culbertson, a graduate of the General Motors Institute (now Kettering) in the late 1970s, says that his era of engineers is being phased out by a new wave of digital engineers who can also design.

"I make good use of a computer, but it's not an appendage," he says. "Computers are just a way of life now. There is a new age of engineer."

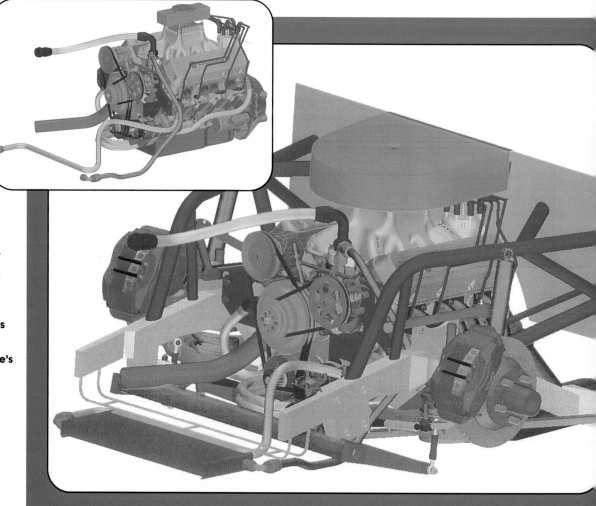

Using Digital Modeling Assembly, the engineering staff at the DaimlerChrysler Tech Center in Auburn Hills, Michigan, can share dimensionally accurate, color-coded representations of the Intrepid R/T Winston Cup car with each of Dodge's five racing teams in North Carolina (far right).

Now more than ever, the changing job description of the engineer has revolutionized the way cars—especially race cars—are built. "In the old days of engineering, it was design it, build it, test it," he says. "Now everything has changed. It's design it, then analyze it."

But even among some of the hottest development technology in the free world, Dodge's entry into NASCAR only revives the age-old debate attacks of other forms of motorsport—such as Formula 1—that the American racing series maintains old technologies in the place of modern-day advancements. Culbertson would like to disagree with those Formula 1 fans, thank you very much.

"NASCAR and Winston Cup is perceived as low-tech, but I totally disagree," he says. "There seems to be two kinds of technology in the world: 'glamorous' technology, which is front-page stuff ranging from traction control to anti-lock brakes to cupholders. But then there is 'non-glamorous' technology, involving stuff like strength of materials, and things like lubricants or reducing weight while maintaining structure. NASCAR racing allows that type of non-glamorous technology to be developed, and these make a difference in the race car. But it means a thousandth of a second. These technologies don't come in and destroy the competition. We have more than 90 percent of our people working on these non-glamorous technologies because they are the most important for what we're doing."

Dodge's engineers still fight to squeeze real track testing for the Intrepid R/T Cup car into the schedule, but they are armed with a host of impressive technologies to speed up the process. After all, how else could they go from zero to Daytona 500 in less than 500 days? ■

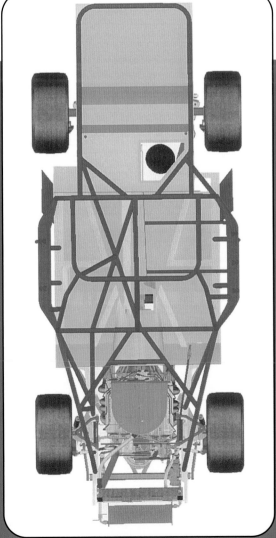

EVERNHAM MOTORSPORTS

By Michael Jordan

Team owner Ray Evernham (below left, with Dodge's Lou Patane) signed 45-year-old NASCAR veteran Bill Elliott and newcomer Casey Atwood, 20, to be his drivers for the 2001 season. Elliott will drive the No. 9 car; Atwood will be behind the wheel of No. 19.

© 2000 ERNEST MASCHE/CIA STOCK PHOTO

ay Evernham is a racer who knows just how important it is to have an edge on the competition. It might have come from his formative years as a drag racer, or perhaps it came from a time as a builder and driver of NASCAR modified cars, but the forty-three-year-old Evernham knows that you can't wait for success to be handed to you. It's the kind of attitude that brought him forty-seven Winston Cup victories and three NASCAR championships in six seasons with Hendrick Motorsports as the crew chief for driver Jeff Gordon, as well as recognition as NASCAR's Winston Cup Crew Chief of the Year in 1994.

Evernham began his career working for Roger Penske, in a shop where the employees all set their watches five minutes ahead as a reminder that timeliness is crucial in racing. And when he undertook the development program for the Dodge Intrepid R/T Winston Cup car on October 14, 1999, Evernham put a clock outside his office to count down the 500 days until the car's scheduled appearance at the 2001 Daytona 500. At the Cup program's announcement, Evernham noted, "Right now I have seven less days than I have miles to compete at Daytona. So we're going to get to work. We plan on unloading at the 2001 Daytona 500, and my goal is to get back to Victory Lane and take the Dodge people with me."

Part of Evernham's edge lies in the recruitment of veteran driver Bill Elliott, who will race in the No. 9 Intrepid R/T. The 1988 NASCAR driving champion

Evernham's cars are sponsored by the 2900 Dodge dealers and the UAW. As the first team owner signed by Dodge to participate in Winston Cup racing, Evernham had less than 500 days to prepare for the 2001 season.

merged his team with Evernham Motorsports, adding not only his experience but also that of his crew in Stateside, North Carolina. At age forty-five, Elliott has 612 career starts in NASCAR's Winston Cup Series and some forty victories. Elliott says, "This gives us the opportunity to make a fresh start with a very high-profile program that all eyes in the racing world will be watching." Evernham says of Elliott, "In addition to being a winner, Bill is the complete package you want in a driver. He's very much into making the car handle, and that's something I'm into as well. We'll be able to communicate and hopefully make rapid progress."

Evernham's second car will be driven by twenty-year-old Casey Atwood. After a youth spent driving go-karts, Atwood graduated to the NASCAR Busch Series in 1998

at age seventeen, becoming its youngest driver ever. He earned his first pole position in that season, and then became the youngest-ever winner in the series a year later. Atwood says of his move to Evernham Motorsports, "I'm really nervous about moving up to Winston Cup. But I know I have the best behind me. I have Ray Evernham, Dodge, and all the Dodge dealers. It's just a great situation." Ray Evernham adds, "A team needs a driver that can tell them what the car is doing, and he's got a tremendous handle on what he needs in a race car."

Lou Patane, vice-president of the Dodge Motorsports operations, says, "When you combine a company with a winning heritage and the resources of Dodge with a proven winner like Ray Evernham, you're going to get a lot done."

PETTY ENTERPRISES

By Michael Jordan

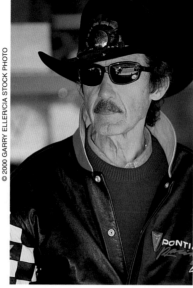

© 2000 GARRY ELLER/CIA STOCK PHOTO

Team owner Richard Petty (above right) and Dodge are together again in Winston Cup racing. Drivers for Petty Enterprises are John Andretti (above), Kyle Petty, and Buckshot Jones, who was named to take the team's vacant seat after Adam Petty was killed during a practice run at the New Hampshire International Speedway.

Surrounded by the woods of Level Cross, North Carolina, Petty Enterprises is just about as far from the elaborate race shops in Charlotte as you can get in modern NASCAR racing. There are twenty-odd buildings here, all the tools of modern stock car racing, and plenty of dedicated people, and yet there's a sense that the down-home roots of NASCAR racing's past are right here.

Maybe it is because Lee Petty began stock car racing right here on the family farm in 1947, preparing his cars in a simple shed propped up by cedar poles. Petty won the NASCAR driving championship in 1954, 1958, and 1959, and his sons Richard and Maurice worked at his side. Together they won the first Daytona 500 in 1959.

Richard Petty began driving on local dirt tracks in 1958 and then went on to win 200 NASCAR races, including seven victories at the Daytona 500. Thanks to engine preparation by Maurice Petty and a crew led by cousin Dale Inman, Richard Petty's Hemi-powered Plymouth GTX won a remarkable twenty-seven races in 1967, including ten in a row. These accomplishments, together with seven NASCAR driving championships, earned Richard Petty recognition as "the King," and his wraparound sunglasses and broad-brimmed Western hat are recognizable to racing fans around the world.

But what makes Petty Enterprises different is the family feeling in the team. Kyle Petty, Richard's son, has carried on the tradition, taking to the race track in 1979 at age nineteen, when he won the Daytona 200 for ARCA

Left: Unpainted, the No. 44, Georgia-Pacific–sponsored Intrepid R/T and the No. 43 Cheerios–sponsored car are prepared for testing in the Petty Enterprises garages in Level Cross, North Carolina. Below: The Petty team's shop.

stock cars in his first-ever major competition. Since then Kyle Petty has won eight NASCAR races. Equally important, he has enhanced the Petty family's strong link with NASCAR fans with countless hours in charitable activities, notably with his cross-country motorcycle rides.

Driver John Andretti also carries the name of a famous family, for he is the nephew of Mario Andretti, the well-known winner of the 1969 Indy 500 (and the not-so-well-known winner of the 1967 Daytona 500). John Andretti began racing midgets while in college, and he has the most varied resume of any NASCAR driver, counting experience in Indy cars, sports cars, and even Top Fuel dragsters. Since his NASCAR Winston Cup debut in 1993 at age thirty, Andretti has won two races.

Buckshot Jones, the newest driver for Petty

Enterprises, has his own family story. While a college freshman, he had a conversation with his father about his ambition to be a NASCAR driver. Together, father and son drafted a five-year plan, which began with the younger Jones's graduation from college and then moved on to an apprenticeship in the NASCAR Busch Series, where he won twice and saw twenty-eight top-ten finishes. At age thirty, Jones is looking forward to being a part of the special spirit that makes Petty Enterprises unique. He says, "To be able to drive for the Pettys and learn from Kyle Petty, Richard Petty, and John Andretti is amazing."

Dodge has a long tradition in NASCAR stock car racing, so it's only natural that it should be affiliated with a team like Petty Enterprises where heritage is an instrumental part of the program.

BILL DAVIS RACING

By Preston Lerner

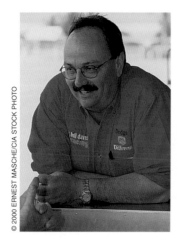

Bill Davis (above) was the third team owner to join the Dodge Winston Cup effort, joining Ray Evernham and Richard Petty. Davis first fielded a team in NASCAR's Busch Series in 1988; he has run Cup cars since 1993.

Ever since he created his race team in 1988, Bill Davis has been a gambler with a keen eye for talent. He's the owner who brought Jeff Gordon to NASCAR, who gave Bobby Labonte his first full-time Winston Cup ride, and who provided the car in which his current driver, Ward Burton, won his first Cup race.

Now Davis is taking his biggest gamble yet—betting that the unblooded Dodge Intrepid R/Ts will be competitive the moment Burton and teammate Dave Blaney unload at Daytona. If they're not, it will be the first big step backward for a team that's gone from success to success over the past decade.

Although Bill Davis Racing doesn't have the cachet of its stablemates, it was the cream of the Dodge crop last year. Burton, overshadowed by brother Jeff, won at Darlington while driving his No. 22 Caterpillar Pontiac to tenth place in the championship. Blaney, meanwhile, finished third in the Rookie-of-the-Year standings in his No. 93 Amoco Pontiac behind the far-better-known Matt Kenseth and Dale Earnhardt, Jr.

Like Burton and Blaney, Bill Davis Racing hasn't gotten the respect it deserves, partly because it's come so far since Davis—the owner of an Arkansas trucking company—built his first Busch Series car in a workshop behind his home, counseled by his friend Mark Martin via nightly long-distance phone calls.

Martin won one race for Davis each of their first three years together in the Busch Series. Davis then scored three more wins in 1992 courtesy of fresh-faced USAC tyro Jeff

Clockwise from far left: Bill Davis Racing's Noel Fulk and Mike Belton adhere decals to driver Dave Blaney's No. 93 Amoco Intrepid R/T; Ward Burton, driver of the No. 22 Caterpillar Intrepid; Davis Racing's head engineer, Todd Holbert, son of three-time Le Mans winner Al Holbert; Davis driver Dave Blaney.

Gordon and then-unheralded crew chief Ray Evernham. In 1993, Davis moved up to Winston Cup, hooking up with Ward Burton in the middle of the 1995 season.

Like Davis, Burton had started at the bottom of the ladder, in his case running the street-stock class at the bullring in his hometown of South Boston, Virginia. Seven races after joining Davis, Burton won at Rockingham, making Davis one of only a handful of owners with Busch and Cup victories to their credit.

During the Nineties, Davis gradually upgraded his team, moving first from his tiny shop in Arkansas to much more spacious digs north of Charlotte and finally a huge state-of-the-art race-shop-cum-tourist-destination in High Point, North Carolina. Meanwhile, the number of Davis employees mushroomed to more than 100.

Among the most important new hires was head engineer Todd Holbert, who provided much-needed technological insight. Then, to further enhance his R&D resources, Davis expanded to a two-car team.

Blaney, a past World of Outlaws champion, was imported to follow the trail blazed a few years earlier by Jeff Gordon. Blaney put in two solid seasons in Busch before graduating to Winston Cup in 2000.

Last year was up and down, with Blaney improving after a rough start and Burton scoring the team's first win—long overdue—since 1995. Both drivers and their respective crew chiefs, Doug Randolph and Tommy Baldwin, return in 2001. Also, the Intrepid R/T promises to be the ace up Davis' sleeve. He may be a gambler, but he likes to stack the deck in his favor.

MELLING RACING
By Michael Jordan

Melling business manager
Lake Speed, Jr. (left) and
crew chief Chad Knaus.

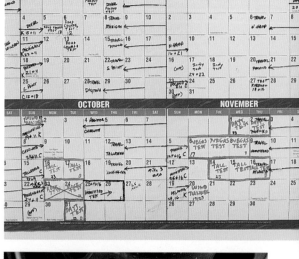

Clockwise, from above: Melling Racing's Skip Pope hand-forms sheetmetal on an English wheel; the Melling team's very full calendar; wheel balancing; a body-builder's set-up sheet.

The late Harry Melling was a man who knew when to take a chance. He helped build his family-owned business, the Melling Tool Company in Jackson, Michigan, into one of the largest suppliers of oil pumps to the automotive aftermarket. After dabbling for years in one-off sponsorships in NASCAR, he decided in 1981 to underwrite the team of three struggling brothers from Georgia—driver Bill Elliott, engine builder Ernie Elliott, and crew chief Dan Elliott. And in 1985, the Elliott brothers brought Melling Racing a remarkable eleven NASCAR Winston Cup victories, while Bill Elliott became the winner of the first Winston Million.

Mark Melling has been in charge of Melling Racing since 1995, when he was just twenty-five. The youngest owner in the NASCAR Winston Cup series, he still has his father's instinct for a likely opportunity. Based in Concord, North Carolina, Melling Racing began upgrading its effort in 2000 by renewing its relationship with engine-builder Ernie Elliott, adding experienced personnel, and moving to larger facilities. And now Melling Racing is a part of the Dodge Intrepid R/T Winston Cup development team.

Driver Stacy Compton understands the advantage that comes from Melling Racing's affiliation with a larger program. He says, "While driving Dodge trucks in the NASCAR Craftsman Truck Series, I experienced first-hand what Dodge wants to do with its One Team concept. All of a sudden we've become part of a multi-car team, and that will allow us to draw on the talent of those other

Below: Chad Knaus (left), crew chief for the No. 92 Kodiak–sponsored Intrepid confers with driver Stacy Compton, who joined Melling's Winston Cup team after a successful stint in NASCAR's Craftsman Truck Series.

teams." Big, multi-car teams hasten the pace of car development, and that represents a big boost for one-car efforts like Melling Racing.

At age thirty-three, Compton illustrates the ability of NASCAR to train younger drivers in its system of junior series. After a youth spent racing go-karts, Compton graduated to the Winston Racing Series in his home state of Virginia, where he won thirty-six times in the early Nineties and qualified on the pole some thirty-nine times. He decided to take a chance in 1996 when he took a one-off Winston Cup drive at Martinsville Speedway, hoping to attract the notice of a top professional team. Once he qualified eighth, he had all the attention he needed, graduating to the NASCAR Craftsman Truck Series. In his two full seasons with the trucks, Compton won twice,

qualified on the pole eight times, and consistently finished in the top ten. He was also part of Dodge's truck effort in 1999, when he recorded six of his runs to pole position in qualifying. Finally Compton came to the Winston Cup Series with Melling Racing at the end of the 1999 season. And his rookie effort in 2000 was marked by an excellent eighth-place start in the NAPA Auto Parts 500 at the California Speedway.

The competitiveness of NASCAR Winston Cup racing has made it harder than ever for small teams like Melling Racing to survive. But with access to first-rate technology afforded by the development program for the Dodge Intrepid R/T, young racers like Mark Melling and Stacy Compton have a chance to show what they can do. And as past experience has shown, all they need is a chance.

CHIP GANASSI RACING WITH FELIX SABATES

By Preston Lerner

Below, left to right: Dodge vice-president Jim Julow, Felix Sabates, Dodge Motorsports vice-president Lou Patane, and Chip Ganassi. Right: NASCAR veteran Sterling Marlin (in race suit). Below right: Ganassi's Andy Graves.

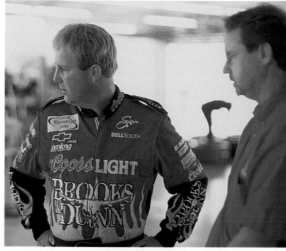

elix Sabates and Chip Ganassi are NASCAR's odd couple. Sabates is a Cuban émigré, Ganassi a Pittsburgh homeboy. Sabates came to racing through business; Ganassi came to business through racing. Sabates is one of NASCAR's most colorful owners; Ganassi made his name—first as a driver, more recently as the series' most successful owner—in CART.

This past year, with four consecutive CART championships under his belt, Ganassi decided to tackle Winston Cup. But instead of creating a team from the ground up—an approach that had yielded disastrous results when CART rival Cal Wells III tried it—Ganassi chose to buy a majority stake in Sabates' operation, Team SABCO. In keeping with their unlikely partnership, the two principals

came up with an equally odd name—Chip Ganassi Racing with Felix Sabates.

Ironically, Team SABCO, like Ganassi's new team, was created by merger rather than out of whole cloth when Sabates bought an R&D operation owned by Rick Hendrick. Sabates quickly established himself as a major player in Winston Cup, with driver Kyle Petty winning seven races for him from 1990 to 1996. In 1994, Sabates opened a magnificent new shop, helping to establish the Garage Majal architectural motif to which all NASCAR teams now aspire.

But the last few years haven't been kind to Team SABCO as drivers came and went without notching any victories. There were high hopes for 2000, which paired six-time Cup race-winner Sterling Marlin with former USAC

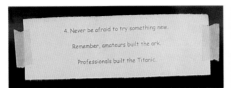

4. Never be afraid to try something new.
Remember, amateurs built the ark.
Professionals built the Titanic.

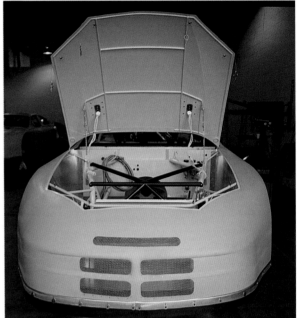

Left: A set of more than twenty rigid aluminum body templates allows NASCAR to legislate aerodynamic consistency among cars in the Winston Cup Series. Above: Engineless and unpainted, one of Ganassi's Intrepids awaits completion.

sprint-car star Kenny Irwin. Instead, the team bottomed out in July when Irwin died in a crash during a practice run at the New Hampshire International Speedway.

By that time, Ganassi had already bought into Team SABCO. Coincidentally, the Chip Ganassi Racing team had followed just the opposite trajectory in CART, finding its feet early in the decade and then dominating at the end, winning championships in 1996, '97, '98, and '99.

Last year, Ganassi and Juan Montoya teamed up to win the Indianapolis 500. Serving as the team manager for that effort was Hendrick Motorsports alumnus Andy Graves, whom Ganassi had hired to run his NASCAR operation. Immediately after the 500, Graves moved to Mooresville and set up Ganassi's Dodge development team in what had been Team SABCO's Busch Series shop.

For 2001, Graves will be joined by the former Team SABCO manager, Tony Glover. Also returning is driver Marlin, driving the No. 40 Coors Light–sponsored car. Marlin gives the new team ties to the hardscrabble roots of NASCAR. His father Coo Coo was a short-track legend. In fact, Sterling ran his first race at age eighteen, when he subbed for his dad at the Nashville Speedway in 1976. He's now best known as a master of restrictor-plate racing, with back-to-back victories in the Daytona 500s of 1994 and 1995.

The team's second seat, in the No. 01 BellSouth Intrepid, remained unfilled well into the off-season. But if his history in CART is any guide, look for Ganassi to hire a rookie—a rookie who, like Ganassi himself, is a very, very quick study.

WHERE THEY RACE

By William Neely

PHOTOGRAPHY BY GEORGE TIEDEMANN

NASCAR race cars roar to tremendous speeds on Daytona's fabled high banks. They muscle their way right back to their roots at short, feisty tracks like Martinsville and Bristol. And they soar into the future at newer tracks such as Texas. The entire racing package offers fans a variety of spine-tingling venues. Here's a sampling of Winston Cup tracks:

DARLINGTON RACEWAY is the granddaddy of stock car superspeedways. In 1950, Harold Brasington carved the high-banked asphalt track out of a cotton field in South Carolina. Fans came from all over the nation to see Darlington's races, and those who couldn't get there snatched up the newspaper the next morning to see what "stock" car had won. For the next year, that particular brand of car was the darling of speed buffs.

The 1.366-mile track is egg shaped for a very good, and very fundamental, reason: There was a swamp on the northwest side of the property and an old-timer's shanty on the southwest side. The man wouldn't budge; nor would the swamp. They didn't have enough land to move the track, so they designed tighter turns at that end, giving it its distinctive look.

Needless to say, it made driving the track at speed, well, awe-inspiring, to say the least. It also gave rise to the moniker: The Track That's Too Tough to Tame.

For the 2001 NASCAR season, the Darlington Raceway will host Winston Cup events on March 18 and September 2.

DAYTONA INTERNATIONAL SPEEDWAY was a marvel from the day the gates were opened in 1959. Nobody had ever seen turns as steep as the 31 degree banking at the splendid Florida speedway. Not only was it the longest track at 2.5 miles, but the mountain-like turns provided a launch pad for unbelievable speeds. The times were so fast, in fact, that something brand new was discovered—drafting. It became an art form in racing.

Cotton Owens turned in the fastest speed in qualifying in 1959 at what fans considered to be just this side of the speed of light, a swift 143.198 miles per hour. Fifty-nine cars lined up for the start of the first Daytona 500, and a new era in stock car racing was born. Twenty-eight years later, Bill Elliott qualified at 210.364 mph.

The Daytona 500 opens the 2001 Winston Cup season on February 18. On July 7, Daytona hosts the Pepsi 400.

LOWE'S MOTOR SPEEDWAY, formerly Charlotte, may well be the most elaborate motor-racing facility in the world. An entire speed city has sprung up around the 1.5-mile, steeply banked (24 degrees) track. Nearly every racing team has its shop and headquarters a mere piston's throw away; not only does a high-rise office tower project from the front straightaway grandstands, but scores of posh condominiums adorn the track's outer perimeter.

The Lowe's Motor Speedway facility is one of the largest sports arenas in the nation, with seating for 167,000 as well as 121 executive suites and room for more than 50,000 additional fans in the infield. Charlotte was the first superspeedway in the country to hold night racing. It also offers dining members a spectacular view of the oval from the Speedway Club, a luxurious environment atop the office tower.

Lowe's Motor Speedway hosts The Winston on May 19, a non-points Winston Cup event. The Speedway's other Cup races are scheduled for May 27 and October 7.

TEXAS MOTOR SPEEDWAY is one of a new wave of racetracks that has sprung up across the country, joining tracks that have been involved in NASCAR racing for more than fifty years. Featuring seating for 150,000 fans, TMS has 194 skybox VIP suites and a front straightaway grandstand that holds 120,000 fans in a section that stretches nearly two-thirds of a mile.

The track, which is near Ft. Worth and on the historic Chisholm Trail, represents the ultimate in luxury and excitement. Speeds on the 1.5-mile, 24-degree banked-turn track are among the fastest in the world, with qualifying speeds exceeding 190 miles per hour (Terry Labonte qualified for the pole of the Texas Motor Speedway's 2000 DirecTV 500 with a speed of 192.137 mph in his Chevrolet).

The Texas Motor Speedway's single Winston Cup event for 2001 takes place on April 1.

INDIANAPOLIS MOTOR SPEEDWAY/ ROGER BEDWELL

INDIANAPOLIS MOTOR SPEEDWAY is at the epicenter of motorsports. Built in 1909, the relatively flat track (turns are banked at 12 degrees, straightaways at 9 degrees) has been home to the Indianapolis 500 since 1911. The 2.5-mile track was originally entirely paved with bricks, giving it the name "Brickyard," but all but three feet of them have been covered over with asphalt, causing the fans to refer to that strip at the start/finish line as the "yard of bricks."

Breaking with its open-wheel tradition, the Indianapo-

lis Motor Speedway added a Winston Cup event in 1994. NASCAR stockers, referred to by locals as "taxicabs" because of their monstrous size compared with the diminutive Indy cars, quickly captured the hearts of even the most die-hard Indy fans.

A reported 300,000 spectators—the largest crowd ever to attend a stock car race—watched as Jeff Gordon captured the inaugural Brickyard 400, and a new tradition was born: stock cars at a track known the world over for open-wheel racers.

The Indianapolis Motor Speedway plays host to the Brickyard 400 on August 5.

BRISTOL MOTOR SPEEDWAY is arguably the fastest half-mile track in the world. With the highest banks in all of NASCAR at 36 degrees, race cars reach unbelievable short track speeds in excess of 125 miles per hour on the concrete surface. Even more astounding is the fact that the half-mile (actually .533 miles) track seats 135,000 people.

The Bristol races are so popular with spectators that tickets are considered to be the hardest to come by in all of racing. Located on the Tennessee side of the border town of Bristol (Main Street separates Virginia and Tennessee), the track opened in 1961 with enough seats for 35,000 fans. It has been in a constant stage of improvement and expansion ever since.

The Bristol Motor Speedway is scheduled to host two Winston Cup races in 2001, on March 25 and August 25.

On August 12, Watkins Glen plays host to the second of the Winston Cup season's two road-race events. The first is at California's Sears Point Raceway on June 24.

WATKINS GLEN INTERNATIONAL is a product of one of the world's oldest road races, dating back to 1948, when sports cars competed on the streets of the village at the southern end of scenic Lake Seneca, one of New York's Finger Lakes.

Over the years, the 2.45-mile course has hosted the United States Grand Prix and many other significant road-racing series. One of only two road courses on the Winston Cup circuit, Watkins Glen features the unusual combination of seven right-hand turns within its eleven corners, which surely is a challenge to drivers who are used to turning left only.

MARTINSVILLE SPEEDWAY is considered by many fans to offer the most aesthetic venue in all of racing, with grass, flowers, a lake with ducks on the property, and a fairly flat half-mile (.526 miles, precisely) track. With tight turns and relatively long straightaways, it's like two drag strips separated by mayhem in the corners. The action is particularly exciting late in the race, by which time many cars have lost their brakes.

The speedway is older than NASCAR itself; it was opened as a dirt track in 1947 by the late Clay Earles, who was one of the most beloved men in the sport, and it has managed to retain the flavor of the earliest days of the sport. One of NASCAR's first heroes, Red Byron, won the first race there in 1947. Byron also won the sixth-ever NASCAR race, held in 1949 at Martinsville. The facility covers more more than 300 mostly manicured acres in Henry County, Virginia, and seats more than 86,000 people.

The Martinsville Speedway's two Winston Cup events for the 2001 season take place on April 8 and October 14.

HISTORY IN ACTION

Making heroes and selling Dodges. By Larry Crane

PHOTOGRAPHY BY DON HUNTER

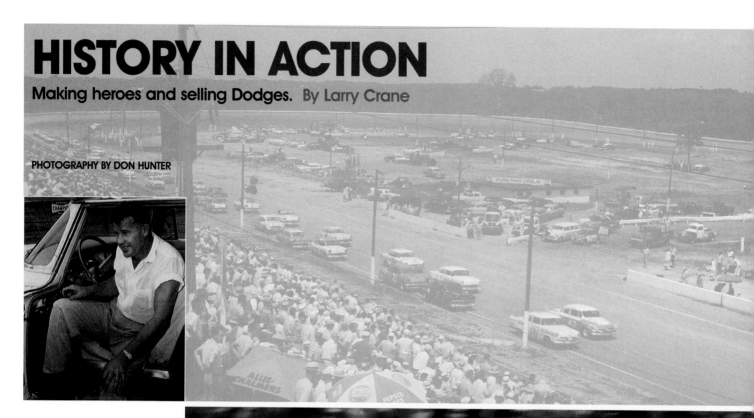

When NASCAR turned 50, so did Petty Racing. Lee Petty (above, and in No. 42, right) founded his dynasty with 54 victories in 16 seasons that included three championships. Lee retired after an accident in 1961, and his son Richard took the wheel. Richard (in No. 43, opposite top, and lost behind Andy Granatelli's celebration in victory circle, opposite) had his first 55 victories in less than eight seasons and went on to 200 wins and seven championships in a career that lasted more than 30 years. His son, Kyle (getting a little mentorship from dad, far right, and in No. 44, facing page), has raced for 20 years. The Petty family has more than 260 Winston Cup wins so far, many of them in Dodges.

DAYTONA RACING ARCHIVES

James Hylton (above) was an independent who raced for points. After 208 races, he had 16 second-place finishes and just one victory. Bobby Allison, in his beautiful 1970 Mario Rossi Dodge (No. 22, right), was a consistent competitor, with 35 percent of his finishes in the top five.

Marty Robbins (wearing helmet, and in No. 42, far left) was a successful singer who raced because he loved it. Buddy Baker (above, and in No. 3, top) had only six victories in 14 seasons. He finished his 326-race career driving a Petty-prepared Dodge and dicing with King Richard.

During the 1970 season, drivers Charlie Glotzbach (above) and Richard Brickhouse (right) were successful in Ray Nichels Engineering–prepared Dodge Charger Daytonas (above right, far right).

Fred Lorenzen (above) had been in retirement for three years when he decided to return to racing. He was leading at Charlotte in May 1970 when his No. 28 Dodge (left) blew on lap 253. Dave Marcis (in No. 30, below) gave Dodge a backup car that was always in contention.

Bobby Isaac drove the
K & K Insurance No. 71
Dodge Charger Daytona
to his 1970 NASCAR
Grand National points
championship. For a more
complete look at this famous
Dodge, turn the page.

THE STUFF OF LEGEND

The high-winged Dodge Daytona
recorded superlatives untouchable until now.

In April 1970, the No. 71 Dodge Charger Daytona sponsored by Nord Krauskopf's K & K Insurance sat on the pole at the Alabama 500, run at the new Talladega Superspeedway. Driver Bobby Isaac achieved a NASCAR record lap of 199.658 mph in the car, which featured an 18-inch bullet nose and a high-mounted rear wing. Isaac went on to take the 1970 Grand National championship with 11 wins and 38 top-ten finishes in 47 races. As an encore, he brought No. 71 back to Talladega and set a closed-course speed record of 201.104 mph. He later drove the car to 28 more speed records at the Bonneville Salt Flats.

PHOTOGRAPHY BY MARK PRESTON

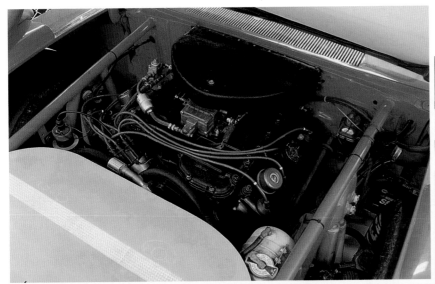

The businesslike interior of No. 71 includes such niceties as a wood dash, a complete set of Stewart Warner gauges, and black carpet. Even at this early stage of development, the "structural" roll cage hinted at NASCAR's evolution from true stock cars to tube-framed racers. The dual rear shocks (top right) were sealed in what appear to be shift boots from an MGB; the differential cooler had its own fan (right).

Above: Mounted two feet above the decklid, the Daytona's rear wing created more than 500 pounds of downforce at race speeds; the reverse-facing scoops on the front fenders were added for tire clearance. When No. 71 was inducted into the National Motorsports Hall of Fame, names of those who had helped make it so winning were painted on its flanks.

Made in
Harrisburg, N.C.

AFTER ALL

DON HUNTER

A U T O G R A P H S

W H O ?
(print person's name here)

WHO?

(print person's name here)

AUTOGRAPHS

AUTOGRAPHS

WHO?

(print person's name here)

WHO?

(print person's name here)

AUTOGRAPHS

AUTOGRAPHS

WHO?

(print person's name here)

AUTOGRAPHS